Picklin' Parson

PICKLIN' WITH PURPOSE™

FROM-THE-FARM GOURMET

Mom and Dad's great room is full of love, and the dining table is overflowing with Honey Onion Chutney.

PICKLIN' PARSON COOKBOOK
When Life Is Jarring, Recipes & Stories to Get Through Tough Times

Publisher's Cataloging-in-Publication Data

Copeland, Stanley R., 1959–
    Picklin' Parson Cookbook, When Life is Jarring, Recipes & Stories to Get Through Tough Times/Stanley R. Copeland

    ISBN   9780578321356

All scripture quotations unless noted otherwise are taken from The New Revised Standard Version (NRSV) and The Message.

A Colinasway Publication

MANUFACTURED IN THE
UNITED STATES OF AMERICA

Table of Contents

Two of my all-time favorite pickle eaters, our granddaughters, Claire Bear and Lily Billy.

Picklin' Parson Cookbook

When Life is Jarring,
Recipes & Stories to Get Through Tough Times

Stanley R. Copeland

When the picklin' and canning party was over at the Holubecs' home, we had a little fun staging this "chutney going to town."

Dedication

This book is dedicated to the volunteers of the relatively new ministry at Lovers Lane United Methodist Church called Food Ministry www.llumc.org/serve. Some of the volunteers of this new ministry have served for the better part of a decade packing food rations through the organization called Feed My Starving Children www.fmsc.org.

For years, our congregation has given generously and has assembled volunteers regularly to pack meals that are delivered to hungry children throughout the world. The organization Feed My Starving Children is simply one of the best to address the issues of hunger among children in dozens of countries around the globe. It distributes millions of nutritious food rations to those in need.

It seems appropriate that a book about recipes for what are largely condiments to larger meals should embrace a purpose of feeding people. First, we can stop and ponder food inequity around the globe and in our communities and what we can do about it. As many of us can choose to top a slab of ribs with chutney, slather apple butter on a piece of toast, or crunch on a pickle, many do not have these privileges of readily available food.

Another thing we can do is pause and thank those who volunteer to serve sisters and brothers who experience food insecurity and those who give generously to such outstanding ministries and organizations that address food-related needs.

In 2020 during the global pandemic as schools and businesses closed, we at Lovers Lane UMC became aware that in our immediate area in Dallas and in neighborhoods throughout the city, people were experiencing food insecurity. This new-to-many term speaks to issues faced largely by the working poor. Many of these sisters and brothers have children who benefit from school breakfast and lunch programs. With schools closed and access to food for children

greatly compromised, churches and other organizations sprang into action. Sack lunches started being delivered to school pickup points, and lines of cars to get these meals quickly grew long. The need was obvious and pressing.

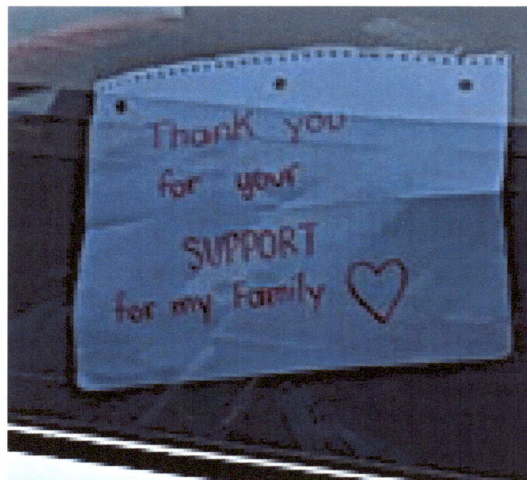

With connections to Shannon and Billy Graham (that's right Billy Graham), owners of Graham's Produce which is not far from the Dallas Farmers Market, Lovers Lane UMC ventured into a ministry we had never attempted. We bought fresh produce and beans made available by Graham's. Tons of rice was provided by another wonderful organization called Rise Against Hunger, through our connection with Jeff Jones who was executive director of this Arlington distribution center at the time www.riseagainsthunger.org.

Soon an army of volunteers met weekly to assemble hundreds of bags full of more than a dozen varieties of fresh vegetables and fruit, rice, and beans. This was enough food for a family to cook several meals and provide nutritious snacks to their children. We set up a distribution spot and an orderly serpentine line of cars filled our large parking lot weekly. We also delivered produce bags to several locations in other neighborhoods, as well as made bags available weekly for some of our own church members. We served—and continue to serve—over seven hundred bags of produce weekly.

The congregation knew in March 2020 that we had no clue that we would be funding such a pressing need that no one anticipated. Tens of thousands of dollars started to flow in to provide this ministry, and the generosity continues. As the 2021 school year starts and the need is still prevalent, our ministry coordinator Randall Lucas reports that over the last seventeen months more than 360 tons of fresh produce, rice and beans was provided to over a quarter of a million individuals (286, 576).

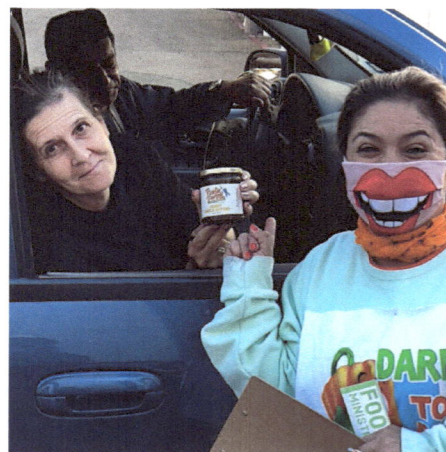

We have received many "thank yous" from those who have received our gifts of food. One thank you was so touching and affirming that we are sharing its goodness with our sisters and brothers. A youth wrote a beautiful letter, accompanied by hand-drawn pictures of the Cuban, Panamanian and American flags.

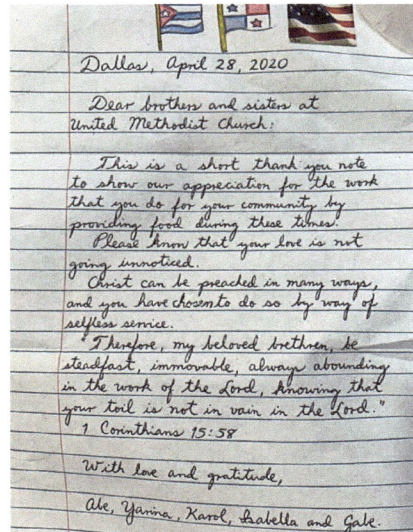

Dallas, April 28, 2020

Dear brothers and sisters at United Methodist Church:

This is a short thank you note to show our appreciation for the work that you do for your community by providing food during these times. Please know that your love is not going unnoticed. Christ can be preached in many ways, and you have chosen to do so by way of selfless service. "Therefore, my beloved brethren be steadfast, immovable, always abounding in the work of the Lord, know that your toil is not in vain in the Lord." I Cor. 15:58. With love and gratitude, Abe, Yamina, Karol, Isabella, and Gabe.

Recently, a jar of blue ribbon-winning Honey Apple Butter was placed in every bag of food distributed from the church. It was labeled: "Loving ALL…You are Loved. A gift of love to you."

To all who have given of their time and money for the sake of others, this cookbook is dedicated in your honor. It's all about the purpose of sharing goodness with others, no matter what.

Others

Charles D. Meigs, 1917

Elizabeth McE. Shields

1. Lord, help me live from day to day In such a self-for-get-ful way That e-ven when I kneel to pray My prayer shall be for— O-thers.

2. Help me in all the work I do To ev-er be sin-cere and true And know that all I'd do for You Must needs be done for— O-thers.

3. Let "Self" be cru-ci-fied and slain And bur-ied deep; and all in vain May ef-forts be to rise a-gain. Un-less to live for— O-thers.

4. And when my work on earth is done, And my new work in Heav-'n's be-gun, May I forget the crown I've won. While think-ing still of— O-thers.

Refrain

O-thers. Lord, yes o-thers, Let this my mot-to be, Help me to live for o-thers, That I may live like Thee.

A Chef's Commendation

Andy Knudson
Chef at Camp Lucy's Tillie's Restaurant
Dripping Springs, Texas

Meet the Chef

The Texas Hill Country, Camp Lucy proudly named award-winning Chef Andy Knudson as the new Executive Chef of their on-property restaurant, *Tillie's* in 2020. Boasting antique architecture, a diverse menu and rich history centered around namesake, Attilia Hancock (a prominent Austin matriarch), *Tillie's* quickly gained traction to become the premier Hill Country dining experience for Dripping Springs residents and Austinites alike. The property's exciting growth paved a welcome for Texas native, Chef Andy Knudson.

Beginning his professional career under the direction of Chef Daniel Boulud, at Restaurant Daniel in New York City, Knudson found his passion for connecting people with warm hospitality and a distinguished menu. Excelling quickly in his craft, he joined the opening team for DB Brasserie at The Wynn Las Vegas Hotel and would eventually move on to 2-Michelin-Star-awarded, Restaurant Guy Savoy.

His subsequent years garnered positions in world-renowned kitchens from coast-to-coast including Aspen's only 5-star hotel, The Little Nell. All the while, Knudson eagerly soaked up the stories of communities in which he cooked, techniques from the professionals from whom he studied, and dreams of the kitchen he hoped to one day run. As fate would have it, a quick vacation would lead him to an introduction to Chef Bobby Flay, where he would become the Executive Sous Chef for Flay's restaurants at Caesars Palace in Las Vegas and Atlantis Paradise Island Bahamas.

Returning to New York City, Knudson found an incredible mentor in celebrity Chef, Marc Forgione. He spent his next five years serving at various Marc Forgione restaurants and was even a member of Forgione's winning team on the popular cooking show, *Iron Chef.* Knudson credits each of the Chefs he has worked alongside for encouraging his exploration of creative freedom in cooking, chasing a higher caliber of clientele, and understanding all components and people that make up the world of food.

In his new role at Tillie's, Chef Knudson will bring a lot more to the table than just delicious food. His methodology centers around international inspiration and an appreciation for the discipline that international cooking embodies. Dining at Tillie's will continue to be an all-senses experience considering everything from the restaurant aroma to presentation and sounds. "Tillie's is for celebrating all things, whether it be life's biggest milestones or simply enjoying the gift of another day," Knudson states.

Chef Knudson aims to tell the story of his travels through the voice of local purveyors. "A meal is much more than the food on your plate. It is a combination of history, cultures, ranchers, farmers and so many more that work together to create what ends up on your table. It is my goal to know the intricate details of where my food is coming from, tell the stories of those growing and raising it, and then share the best of the Hill Country in ways it has yet to be explored," said Knudson.

Lastly, with acknowledgment of the culture that life in the kitchen can foster, Knudson shares, "I want my team to be a professionally-trained kitchen and have the skill set to pursue their passions. However, it is equally as important for me to support them in their growth and ensure a healthy environment for them to do so." When asked what he hopes to accomplish in this new role, Knudson replied, "I look forward to sharing stories with our guests over the dinner table and building upon the incredible story that is Tillie's Restaurant."

Chef Meets the Picklin' Parson

Chef Andy Knudson states, "When I first met Stan "Picklin Parson" Copeland I was traveling back and forth to visit family living in Aspen Colorado. Went to several services he was leading and felt a real connection. Over the years we had met and spoke about life, food and family, as our friendship grew.

In 2017, we asked if he would be the officiant at our wedding. Gladiz and I were excited that not only would he do the wedding, but we commissioned Stillwater Farm Market Store, of which he is an owner, to make the delicious, homemade, specialty ice cream. Yes, that's right the Picklin' Parson makes ice cream too.

Since that time, our families become even closer, and we talk a lot about a mutual love--food.   More than that we talk about not wasting fresh from the farm produce, and preserving fresh fruit and vegetables, even the no-so-pretty stuff. `Chefs Secret' the ugly vegetables taste as good or better than the pretty ones at the store. Picklin' and canning as he calls it, is all about preserving the best of flavors and makes that which is jarred beautiful, from whatever point of beauty it started.

One of the missions that I have in my restaurants is minimal waste. At camp Lucy we have laying chickens that we feed all of the vegetable scraps to and then they give us eggs in return, with which we make pasta dough. When we are not taking the trim we are making pickles, chutney or just preserving the vegetables that we get for menu items that we will put on in the winter months. I always tell the team spring and summer can last all year if you just put it in a jar. And that is what the Picklin' Parson's cookbook is all about, "putting it in a jar."

/tär 'tär/

adjective [after noun]

In the United Kingdom and New England, it is pronounced

/tä 'tä/

(Of fish or meat) served raw, typically seasoned and shaped into small cakes.

Tartar is a fish or meat that is cut into very small pieces and served without being cooked. This is a dish that I can make over and over and never change. The beauty of making a tartar is that you are not wasting those end cuts whether it is land animal, or seafood (I do not recommend chicken).

Chop the fish or meat up very finely and just add what you need. Adding an array of flavors from the recipes in this cookbook is simply adding delicious acid. Pick a chutney, any chutney and see what it's like. You could also season with a vinegar or FRESH citrus, please don't use the pre-packed stuff. As I have been told my entire career, "If you don't try you don't know!" Bon appétit! Chef Andy Knudson

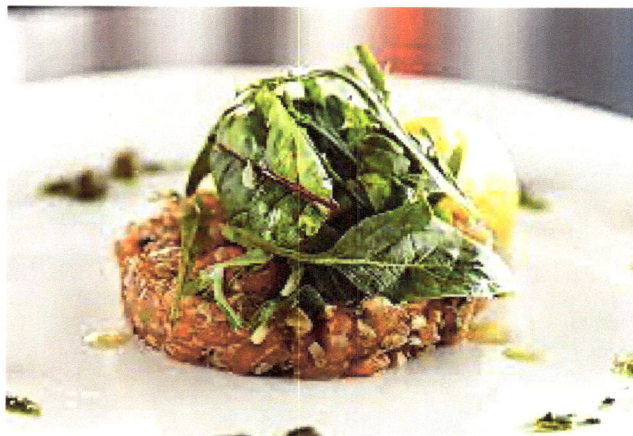

Award-Winning
From-the-Farm Gourmet Jars of Goodness

Blue Ribbon – 1st Place

1. Aunt Rose's Marinated Mixed Veggies –   State Fair of Texas 2020

2. Bango Mango Chutney –   North Texas State Fair 2021
   East Texas State Fair 2021

3. Blueberry Thyme Jam –   West Texas State Fair 2021
   (contender for best of show)
   3rd North Texas State Fair 2021
   3rd East Texas State Fair 2021

4. Carnival Apple Butter   East Texas State Fair 2021

5. Cinnamon-Spiced Peppered Peaches –   East Texas State Fair 2019

6. Garlic Pickled Asparagus   East Texas State Fair 2021

7. Garlic Pickled Okry –   State Fair of Texas 2020
   3rd North Texas Fair 2021
   East Texas State Fair 2021

8. Ginger-Spiced Peppered Pears –   State Fair of Texas 2021
   3rd East Texas State Fair 2019
   3rd East Texas State Fair 2021

9. Ginger Tomato Chutney –   North Texas Fair 2021
   West Texas State Fair 2021

10. Gran's Pear Honey –   East Texas State Fair 2019

11. Honey Apple Butter –   North Texas State Fair 2021
    West Texas State Fair 2021

12. Honey Onion Chutney –

East Texas State Fair 2021
North Texas Fair 2021
2nd State Fair of Texas 2021
West Texas State Fair 2021

13. Lemon Elephant Garlic –

State Fair of Texas 2021
3rd East Texas State Fair 2021

14. Mamma Hacy's Lemon Figs –

East Texas State Fair 2021
North Texas Fair 2021
HM State Fair of Texas 2020

15. MawMaw's Virginia Chunk Sweet Pickles –

North Texas Fair 2021
West Texas State Fair 2021
East Texas State Fair 2021

16. Ol' Timey Pear Mincemeat –

West Texas State Fair 2021
2nd State Fair of Texas 2020

17. Salty Dog Dills –

North Texas State Fair 2021
East Texas State Fair 2021

18. Strawberry Basil Jam –

West Texas State Fair 2021
2nd North Texas Fair 2021
3rd East Texas State Fair 2021

19. Triple-Play Pickled Garlic –

North Texas State Fair 2021
West Texas State Fair 2021
3rd State Fair of Texas 2021
2nd East Texas State Fair 2021

Red Ribbon – 2nd Place

1. Amaretto Cherries –

State Fair of Texas 2021
West Texas Fair 2021
3rd North Texas Fair 2021

2. Sage Blackberry Chutney –

North Texas Fair 2021
3rd East Texas State Fair 2021

3. Mint Cilantro Relish –   North Texas Fair 2021

4. Brandy Peach Chutney –   North Texas Fair 2021
                                             3rd East Texas State Fair 2021

5. Pecan Praline Figs –   East Texas State Fair 2019
                                             <mark>HM State Fair of Texas 2019</mark>

White Ribbon – 3rd Place

1. Minty Green Apple Chutney –   North Texas State Fair 2021

2. Moonshine Vanilla Peach Jam –   East Texas State Fair 2019

3. Raspberry Mint Jam –   North Texas State Fair 2021
                                             East Texas State Fair 2021

4. Trinity Savory Okra--   State Fair of Texas 2020

Recipe to Read

Reading a Picklin' Parson cookbook is an odd and exciting undertaking, for the book has narrative for the purpose of pondering stories, questions, poems, and life situations that very well might coincide with the reader's experiences. The title, When Life is Jarring, Stories and Recipes to Get Through Tough Times says it all. All of us have jarring experiences, the hope for the reader is that this cookbook will be a pick-me-up and a refocusing on the joys of life. The larger purpose is: *"Joyfully connecting people by sharing the art of picklin' and canning from-the-farm gourmet goodness."*

This cookbook on the art of pickling and canning farm-fresh goodness in fruits and vegetables contains twenty-three pages of introduction. There are six stories and sixteen pickle, chutney, jam, jelly, and butter recipes. There are also seven recipes of dishes that the from-the-farm goodness in jars can enhance. Definitions of the categories—pickles, chutneys, herbed jams & jellies, and spiced butters also are featured. There are Appendices A and B that explain the equipment and process of water bath canning and an old family fermenting recipe for brining and crisping pickles. There are also over one hundred photos. Oh yeah, and cherries on top at the end.

Ingredients

- Picklin' Parson's Cookbook 2022: When Life is Jarring
- Favorite beverage in a special mug or glass
- Great spot to read and meditate

Steps

1. In the first session, introduce yourself to the cookbook by reading the first 23 pages.
2. In the following sessions, read each story in one 20 to 30-minute session at a time at a welcoming spot with a favorite beverage. Enjoy!
3. Remember the light grey shaded boxes is content or questions for you to ponder.
4. Skim the recipes as you go through the stories.
5. After reading the stories, read about each of the categories and the recipes in each segment. Spend about 20 or 30 minutes in these sessions.
6. Spend a session reading Appendices A and B to learn more about the art of pickling and canning and the old recipe for brining and crisping pickles.
7. In a couple of weeks over five to seven hours, you will have read and contemplated the contents of the entire book.

NOTE: There will be a future audiobook that I will read for your enjoyment.

An Opening Word
Dr. Stanley R. Copeland, The Picklin' Parson
Lovers Lane United Methodist Church
Dallas, Texas

It is somewhat ironic that for this rural East Texas guy, urban settings have largely been my pastoring perches for the better part of four decades.

The last twenty-four years I have been the pastor in Dallas, Texas at a church named Lovers Lane United Methodist Church. Lovers Lane is a funny name for a church that is no longer on the street called Lovers Lane, but the connection to love is a powerful one since the mission of the church is "Loving ALL..." Lately, somewhat jokingly, someone called me the Picklin' Parson. Another funny name. "Why Picklin' Parson?" you might ask. Therein lies the story that I desire to share.

My name is Stan Copeland, and I love my roles as husband, father, grandfather, uncle, cousin, friend, and pastor — or as a friend of mine loves to call me "parson." I was ordained in the United Methodist Church in 1983, but preached my first sermon in 1975, at the age of sixteen, to my home church in Chandler, Texas.

Putting It on the Table

First, let me get something on the table besides pickles, chutneys, jams, jellies, and butters. I am used to parsons being perceived as "killjoys" and "duds." There is a part of me that works hard to dispel those labels. For that matter, Christians are viewed today by many as judgmental and exclusive folks. I believe we followers of Jesus must prove this perception wrong by our actions of love and inclusion of all in the spirit of Jesus who we uplift. I see no viable future for any Christian congregation or denomination that excludes people— especially if the Bible is used to justify the action.

I've heard testimonies from people who believe they are God-led to professions like physician, attorney, politician, domestic worker, teacher, police officer, garbage collector and armed services personnel, as well as clergy. It's my belief that no profession is valued by God over another. It's all a matter of what our God-led faith compels us to do and to whom our faith directs our paths.

I realize that some reading this book may not profess faith at all and are wondering what on earth is up with picking up a parson's book on picklin' and canning. If that describes you, I hope you will read it and know that I am most honored by your attention to the book with its story-laced recipes.

The best of life is about being people of purpose and meaning, committed to making a difference for the good and well-being of others, along with the globe that we share. In whose name you live and act is your business. I aspire to be an open-minded and open-hearted Christian pastor who is principled and purposed by Jesus. I greatly value and engage the Bible, and question narrow interpretations of it. That is my business. In these pages, far be it from me to force any unwanted business on anyone.

This is by no means a "preachy book," but one that intends to lift up the art of pickling and canning of vegetables and fruit. It also contains recipes and stories that are about people, relationships and life that comes our way. It is fitting to say it is a cookbook with a purpose of inspiring toward hope and a deep-seated happiness. Perhaps some will try their hand at picklin' and canning or pick it back up after years of dormancy. My wish is that the words on these pages will move readers to be more respectful, kind and loving in their relationships and conversations—and that these connections move them to be more hopeful when life is jarring.

Picklin', Parson, and Purpose

I am a country boy at heart and my pickling and canning connects me to my family. As a boy, I watched with curiosity as my grandmothers and mother pickled and canned. The amazing results of this busyness was delightful and delicious.

Let's start this saga with pickling. Picklin' is the way we East Texans say "pickling," which refers to the art of water bath canning of vegetables and fruit. It also leans into the canning of chutneys, jams, jellies, butters, and preserves. "Parson" is the title that is a more antique version of "pastor." In East Texas the word "preacher" is also ascribed to the same role as a parson, acknowledging the activity of proclaiming the good news of our faith, which many see as my job.

"Picklin' with a purpose" is all about connections. The ultimate good news of faith is about connecting us to the abundance of God's love, joy, and peace—abundant life. In that same spirit, we are connected to family, friends and those who come our way. For this parson, picklin' becomes a means to the purposeful end of "joyfully connecting people to one another by sharing the art of pickling and canning from-the-farm gourmet goodness."

It is my experience that whether we are connecting with people through picklin' and canning in a home or discussing the stories in a Picklin' Parson cookbook with a group of people, new conversation arises. The information found in the shaded boxes is meant to be pondered. By "ponder" I mean think, remember—even meditate or pray. My prayer is that by engaging in this agrarian art, it can be a simple way to connect people to a greater purpose and deepen relationships. May we all be committed to meaningful unity (not uniformity) and to wholesome, new conversation. May abundant living be brought into focus as a gift to us from a gracious and loving higher power as we read, listen, and ponder.

Jarring and Redemption

The *"Picklin' Parson Cookbook When Life is Jarring, Stories & Recipes to Get Through Tough Times"* gets at a universal dynamic of the human condition—namely painful or jarring life experiences. It's obvious by now

> *Jesus said, "I came that you may have life, and have it abundantly." John 10:10*

that the Picklin' Parson is bent toward turning a phrase. Using a word with at least a double meaning—like "jarring"—is intentional, evoking a deeper importance. Moving the reader to stories and recipes is met with the hope of joy being ushered into every heart.

Addressing the art of picklin' and canning causes me to confess that nothing in the process goes into a can. Pickles, jams, jellies, and the like find their way into jars like the classic ones called "Mason." Technically, the Picklin' Parson really pickles and jars. When it is said that something is jarring, the reference is to a circumstance that is unsettling, shocking, and usually entails loss is a reminder that life is sometimes jarring. The jarring can be the loss of: a loved one to death, a relationship to divorce, a home and possessions to fire or weather, freedom to poor choices, hopes and dreams to uncontrollable circumstances and unity to conflicts and war. The jarring or canning of vegetables and fruit—or as I like to say, "farm-fresh goodness"—is completely different. At best, the cookbook juxtaposes purposeful abundant life through Godly connections to any loss that may come our way.

The underlying belief is that God desires to redeem the worst of jarring circumstances that we may face, and I testify to being a witness to such redemption.

Laments to Good News

When I was being trained to preach in seminary, I was taught to create a sermon with the end in mind. Ultimately, you must consider where you are going before you ever start and always end up with the Good News on the pedestal. It is not lost on me that collectively—as a global community—we have faced one of the

> *Post-COVID-19, How do you think that life will be changed? What differences do you anticipate in the workplace, families, and churches?*

most jarring times in our history that has been brought on by the worldwide pandemic named COVID-19.

This global challenge came to be in 2019 and still impacts lives throughout the world. As I imagine picklin' and canning with you, spinning stories, and pointing toward truth, please know that COVID-19 and divisions that have been magnified by its presence will NOT have the last word.

Laments continue in many forms and words of church members surface around the theme "Will life and church ever be as they once were?" As one charged to herald the Good News—being informed by the reality of my faith—my answer is emphatically, "No!" Life and the life-changing fellowship of the church are being redeemed by God, who is good all the time. I believe we can be better than ever been before.

Preserving and Sharing

Let us not forget that the ultimate purpose of the simple art of picklin' and canning is "preservation." Keeping that which is placed into jars good and wholesome is the intended result. There are those good and life-giving aspects of living that will continue to be preserved. According to Galatians 5:22-23, "The fruit of the Spirit is love, joy peace, patience, kindness, generosity, faithfulness, gentleness and self-control." These are some of those things that make for the good life and wholesome living.

Finally, I remember from times past—and practice today—the act of sharing the created goods with friends, neighbors, and even strangers as a gesture of love and care. After canning fig preserves, sweet chunk pickles, or pear honey, I can hear my grandmothers saying, "I'm going to take a jar of pickles to Aunt Minnie. She hasn't been feeling well," "That new man in town needs a jar of figs to know we are neighborly, and that we're glad he is here," or "Alice — with that new baby and the other two little ones — might find a jar of pear honey just what she and the kids need right now on their biscuits."

Today, we share jars of apple butter and other delightful, jarred goodies with homebound members, friends who visit our fellowship, persons recently discharged from hospitals, people needing prayers who members tell us about, and strangers we are made aware of who may have a need for a special act of kindness. The recipients love the gestures, as well as the contents in the jars. The ones who get to deliver the gifts know the purposeful joy and abundant life involved in giving.

How can such a simple act of sharing with neighbors be so fulfilling and spiritually satisfying? I think it goes back to what French Jesuit priest and theologian Pierre Teilhard de Chardin said, "We are not human beings having a spiritual experience; we are spiritual beings having a human experience."

Sharing is also at the heart of the spirituality that this book is about. What a joy it is to share these recipes and stories, as well as let you in on the greater purpose—which in a word is "sharing." If you try your hand at picklin' and canning and come up with some jarred goodness, share it as a gift of love. It's like a magic penny. You know the little children's song?

Love is something if you give it away, give it away, give it away.
Love is something if you give it away. You'll end up having more.
It's just like a magic penny. Hold it tight and you won't have many.
Lend it, spend it, and you'll have so many. They'll roll all over the floor.
Love is something if you give it away, give it away, give it away.
Love is something if you give it away. You'll end up having more.

The food life of any party—chutney and cheese. Ponder what Jesus said, "The Son of Man has come eating and drinking, and you say, `Look, a glutton and a drunkard, a friend of tax collectors and sinners!" Luke 7:34

Story One

Jarring to Joy

One never knows what a day will bring, ascending to the highest mountain of joy can quickly descend to the lowest valley of jarring loss.

In August 2017, our youngest child, Emily, got married at our church in Dallas. All our family was present at the wedding, including my mom, who was greatly compromised by Parkinson's disease. She had bravely faced it for the better part of thirty years. Nothing was going to keep her away from her youngest granddaughter's wedding.

Having Moppie and Poppie—as my parents are affectionately called—at the wedding rehearsal on Friday evening and the wedding and reception on Saturday was remarkable. It was the first time they had been away from their home for two consecutive nights in years. Our extended family had come in from different parts of the state and country, and we were all staying in the same hotel in downtown Dallas. What a gift it was to share this time together.

The wedding was beautiful and with only the reception downtown to come afterwards, we left the church and headed for the heart of downtown Dallas. Over a year of planning was fast approaching "done." During the reception we all marveled at the spectacular storm and lightning display that we could see across the city as we faced east. After the reception was over, guests had gone home; what took months to plan had transpired perfectly. Tammy and I retired to our hotel room with a big, satisfied sigh.

Fiery Storms of Life Come

I had just sat down and taken off my shoes when my dad phoned me from his room a few doors away. He said, "Bub, we just got a call from Chandler. (pause) Our home was struck by lightning, and it has burned to the ground. Everything is lost. It's all gone." Disbelief and dumbfounded chatter between the two of us allowed the harsh reality to begin to sink in. The trip from a pinnacle of satisfaction and joy to the hell of a shock, accompanied by despair and loss, was truly jarring. I had questions, but the most important one was how was Mom, and if she knew the devastating news. He said that she was asleep, and he thought he'd wait until morning to tell her.

We formulated a plan to convey the difficult words before engaging in a very sleepless night. The next morning, my sister Jill and brother-in-law Kyle, my wife Tammy and our entire family gathered in my parents' hotel room to share the heartbreaking news with our Moppie. All our family was there—except for honeymoon-bound Emily—who we somehow kept from knowing in this day of rampant social media.

I'll never forget the poignant scene of our dad kneeling in front of our mom who was in her wheelchair. Surrounded by all our family, Dad said, "Marty," which only he called her. Looking eye-to-eye, he paused. Then he said, "I have some bad news. Our house was struck by lightning last night in the storm and has burned to the ground. Everything is gone."

Mom hung her head and started to cry softly, as we all teared up. Then she said with a hint of a question as she was leaning toward resolve, "All our things?" Sobs began to surface. She cried for only a few seconds before she broke the sobbing and looked around at all of us and said, "But we have each other, and that is the most important thing. We have our family. And we are safe." By this time, Dad was crying too. Mom then looked directly into his eyes and said, "Don, it's going to be okay. We'll all be fine. God will take care of us.

We will be just fine. We have our family." Then she looked around at all of us and said, "I love all of you." The one to be consoled had become the "consoler-in-chief," which was true to form.

The next morning, we ate breakfast at the hotel, with family checking to see if we were OK, given the circumstances. Then we made the 90-mile trip to Chandler and the smoldering ruins that was once a beautiful home on the farm. Dominant in my mind was the thought that we would never again gather in the family room to behold the one-hundred-year-old drugstore fountain with the marble bar, full of family history. My grandfather Copeland who originally owned the fountain, owned a drugstore in West Texas before buying the drugstore in Chandler. My father and sister are also pharmacists. The antique piece of furniture framed so much conversation and laughter. Now it was gone, lost to the flames.

We arrived and got out of our vehicles to ponder the present and allow "loss" to sink in as much as possible. The sight of coming down the lane to only the natural beauty of the farm with no house prominently standing was an overwhelming emotional experience that will live with me all my life.

Containers of Family Treasures

In her healthier days, Mom was an avid collector. She loved to save family relics in plastic containers that were dated by year and perpetually held treasures i.e., funeral bulletins, awards, newspaper clippings and photos—lots of photos. She poured over the contents in each container, sorted, remembered, slightly reconfigured, and placed them back in their cubbies. She so thoroughly enjoyed time with the family treasures. All were gone, except the memories, and the jury was out on whether the joy would ever return. Would joy be lost to terminal heartache? Feelings were still too raw to judge the future.

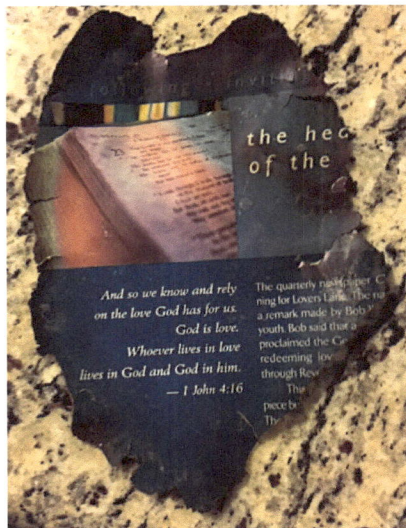

Suddenly through my teary eyes, I saw a piece of paper floating up in the air and gently sinking down before resting on the toasted grass. The singed page tossed and turned once or twice in the summer morning breeze before I curiously snagged it. I recognized it immediately as a burned portion of a Lovers Lane UMC church newsletter that Mom had saved. On the blackened page of the newsletter, all that was left, were these words of I John 4:16.

> *"And so, we know and rely on the love God has for us. God is love. Whoever lives in love lives in God, and God in them."* I John 4:16 NIV

Could it be that the Holy Spirit was reminding us that God's love would see us through, just as Moppie had proclaimed a few hours earlier? We all prayed it would be so. A few days later, God's love showed up and showed out.

> **When has God's love showed up and showed out, seeing you through a jarring circumstance?**

The decision had been made to raze the slab and remove all the debris. Individuals from the community of Chandler and its United Methodist Church arrived to do the laborious task on the appointed day. Soon cars from Dallas with members of Lovers Lane UMC arrived and began to unload. They introduced themselves to my parents and new fellow laborers and friends. Our congregation in Dallas is very multicultural, particularly featuring members from the continent of Africa.

We all gathered around Dad before starting to work on the still smoldering mess. "Ol' Don from Chandler" — as he customarily introduces himself — thanked us for coming with his familiar smile and country drawl. He then called on his pastor, Bryan Harkness, to pray before we started our day together—rural and urban, black and white, U.S. citizens and immigrants. Not all of us were of the same Christian faith expression or theological opinion, yet we were all speaking the same language— LOVE—in an array of dialects.

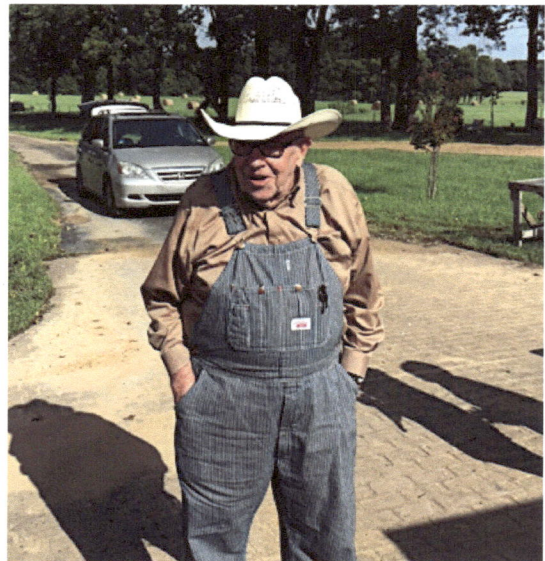

The dominant dialect was East Texan. The Africans could understand East Texan because they had been listening to me for years. We were united by our purpose and convened by the Spirit of love, joy, and peace. We prayed to the One we knew and on whom all relied—especially in times like these. In two days, the slab was cleared, and the rubble was interred in the sandy loam and blood-orange clay soil of the farm.

Rebuilding Plans Underway

Mom and Dad lived for six weeks with her only sister, Alice Wilson, who was eighteen years her junior. They had been sisters for more than six decades but until now had never lived under the same roof for any length of time. It was so healing for Mom and Dad to be cared for so well by Alice, who had buried her own husband just weeks before.

During this time, we had secured Mom and Dad a home in Chandler across from their beloved First United Methodist Church. I say, "we" because some of my dear friends went together with me to get a line of credit for the purchase that we would repay when the new house was built, and the house in town sold. It worked perfectly. Mom and Dad settled comfortably in the town where they had lived for over eighty years.

Our son Zachary is an architect, and he worked hard on designing a new house for his grandparents, overseeing its construction. The plan was to build the new house right on the spot where the old house stood. Autumn came and gave rise to winter. January brought the beginning of building and the birth of Claire Marie Copeland. This little one was our son Zach's and daughter-in-law Emily's first baby. Between a new baby and designing a house, it was a very busy time for Zach to say the least. Claire Bear was Moppie and Poppie's fourth great grandchild.

Winter yielded to spring, and the summer brought forth vegetables and fruit, especially figs. Our family loves figs. When I say, "our family," I am connecting with great-great-grandparents, great-grandparents, grandparents, aunts, uncles and cousins—all who lived in this East Texas area and engaged in rural living.

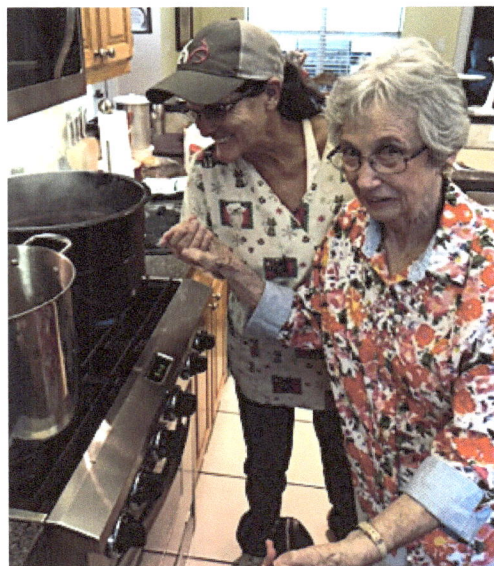

I had the big idea to follow through on a plan that I had pondered for several years, which was trying my hand at pickling and canning. My hope was that it would lift my mom's spirits to cook and water-bath can some fig preserves. I imagined them going into Mason jars—according to her grandmother Mamma Hacy's Lemon Fig Preserves recipe—and looking beautiful.

I bought a canning pot and a stockpot, along with the rest of the equipment and items needed for the task of canning preserves. Mom seemed to be game to coach, as her friend and caregiver, Tina, assisted me in this maiden canning voyage. It surprised me how much

fun we had in the process. I asked Mom questions about her grandmothers and mother and what she remembered about their "picklin' and canning." She was full of information and eager to provide details about generations of wholesome family and community life.

When a few hours had passed, and Mom—being the cooking coach—said that figs had reached the mark of being done, we ladled them into their jars for sealing. The water in the canning pot was boiling and ready to receive the jars, bringing completion to the process. After a dozen minutes in the gently boiling water, they were taken from the water bath jar by jar and placed on a towel on the kitchen bar. We waited for them to cool and anticipated the lids popping and pinging as if to say, "Done!" Mom smiled and said, "They look just like Mamma Hacy's figs." She seemed so pleased and taken back to a family time, a healthier time. I could not have been happier. We had gone from shocking, jarring news to a delightful, peaceful jarring pastime.

Most notably, the little brown fruit delights tasted like the lemon fig preserves passed down through the generations to this point in precious time. Joy was in the air, and I was so happy with the results of a newfound hobby. I spent the summer of 2018 canning fig preserves, praline fig jam, strawberry fig jam, and even pickled some peaches.

Home Sweet (Pickle) Home

On August 30, 2018, one year and two weeks since the fire destroyed their home, Mom and Dad were home again in a grandson-designed space. Their new, beautiful home had a gorgeous, spacious kitchen featuring a huge island counter that Mom could easily walk around and hold onto, if she needed to steady herself. She could even ride around

it on her mobile wheelchair. The loveliest view in the house was at the kitchen sink that looked out over the pine-tree-sprinkled hay meadow and beyond to an eight-acre lake. The kitchen was a perfect place for pickling and canning.

One of Mom's first cousins, Margaret Ann Ellis Spruill, sent Mom and Dad a quart jar of MawMaw Ellis' Virginia Chunk Sweet Pickles as a housewarming gift. She also sent us a jar of the sweet pickles, and they were delicious. With the recent success of canning the fig preserves, I was tempted to continue to try my hand at picklin' and canning. Sweet pickles were now in my sight. I asked Margaret Ann for MawMaw Ellis' recipe, and she gladly delivered.

M'lisa Ellis or MawMaw Ellis was my great-great-grandmother, and she died when I was eight years old. It is not lost on me how unusual it is for me to say that I knew two of my great-great-grandmothers, three of my great-grandmothers, and two of my great-grandfathers. Both my maternal and paternal grandparents were a very important part of my life growing up. A great blessing of my life has been rural living around extended family. We are not related to everyone in our little town, but we could once call more than half the population of Chandler "cousin."

MawMaw's sweet pickle recipe was a challenge and required fruit-of-the-Spirit patience. It took twelve days to make! For seven days, the fresh cucumbers sat in a crock full of brine that shriveled and wrinkled them as they fermented. On Day Eight they were chunked, sliced in unequal pieces, and transferred to a hot crisping solution. For the next two days, the pickles were drained, and new crisping solution was reapplied. The spicing began on Days Eleven and Twelve. On Day Thirteen, the sweet pickles were placed into jars with their sweet, spice-rich syrup poured over them. Then finally, they were water-bath canned.

My first attempt was a surprising success. The pickles were amazingly delicious and just the way I remembered them tasting at family meals and holiday feasts of days gone by. The sweet pickles were so crisp that you could snap them like a fresh potato chip. All was well and felt settled. The great jarring experience of the house fire—along with personal possessions destroyed in the fire—seemed to have been redeemed.

The Jarring Loss of Megan

In May 2019, our family was jarred again with a stage-four cancer diagnosis of our niece Megan. The cancer that had spread terribly and thoroughly throughout her body was prone to take her precious life. Never had we faced such a challenge with one of our immediate family. Coach Megan—seemingly the healthiest of us all—was the last one we expected to be facing such a jarring battle.

If you didn't know Megan, I am sorry; she was pure, unadulterated joy. Her face always glowed with a beautiful smile, and she was a blessing to so many. Full throttle was her life pace with a passion for faith, family, community, and team. She was a daughter, sister, granddaughter, niece, cousin, wife, mom, friend, and coach. Those were her roles in life that she played with great resolve and satisfaction. When one saw her smiling face, smiling back was the only appropriate response. And that smile attracted people of all ages to her like a magnetic force.

Her athletic ability was only topped by her incredible people skills and relational nature, which made her a great coach. We still miss her every day since she outran us to heaven on August 14, 2019. We will never forget her. Slowly but surely our memories are bringing to bear the joy of the blessing of her life, rather than the overwhelming grief of our incredible loss.

Six months before Megan was born, I was diagnosed with leukemia that was expected to be terminal within three years. There was no treatment or cure at the time for the kind of leukemia I had contracted. I will share more about this aspect of my life in the final story of the cookbook. As you have probably figured out, here I still am forty years later. I have my own questions for God to which I know the Great Healer will be able to account for. My questions are not driven by doubt. Rather, they are about a need for personal peace regarding why young people like Meg acquire cancer and some succumb to it while others survive its death grip.

My mentor the Reverend Dr. Bill Hinson's words always ring in my ears, "I pray to a God who heals. Some of us may be healed miraculously and will have to find out what really happens when we get to heaven. Some of us may be healed like the Apostle Paul who prayed for the 'thorn in his flesh' to be removed, and it wasn't. Yet he could say, *'God's grace is sufficient to supply all my needs.'* ALL of us are healed on the other side of the Jordan in that land that knows no night, where there is no more weeping and pain. The land that is eternal in the heavens is our ultimate healing destination."

We prayed and hoped against hope that Megan would be gifted that miracle of healing and be cured. It was a strength-sapping summer as she declined so decisively before our eyes. Her family and friends sat with her—person by person, by her bed every minute—every day until her earthly end and her eternal beginning.

Sweet Megan has her place in that land that is eternal in the heavens. I am so very grateful for her life. Our loss was—and is—very real, but Megan is not lost. By faith, we know exactly where she is.

The Bite of the Picklin' Bug

In the middle of such a stressful and sad time, the picklin' bug bit me hard and decisively, and now it had the cathartic dynamic of solace. I decided to submit entries to the State Fair of Texas. Some entries were from recipes that had been passed down for generations. Others were my own recipes. Some of the entries I cooked with Mom by my side in her new house, in that beautiful kitchen of which she was so proud.

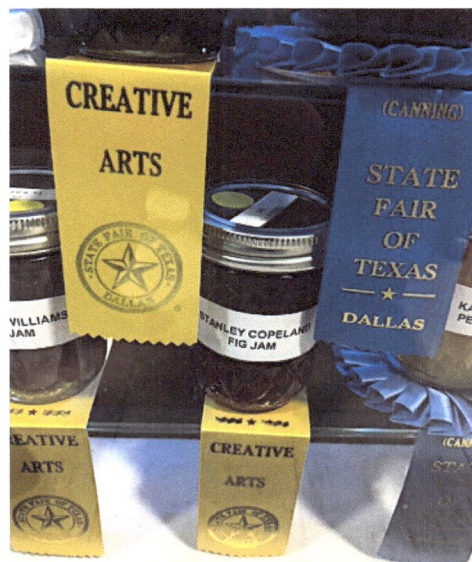

In the 2019 State Fair of Texas, I had five entries, including the only award winner. The Praline Pecan Figs won an Honorable Mention or fourth place. I entered six jars of farm-fresh goodness in the 2019 East Texas State Fair, and wow, was I shocked at the success. Ribbons galore! There were two blue ribbons for Gran's Pear Honey and Cinnamon Spiced Jalapeno Peaches. Two red, second-place ribbons came my way for Mamma Hacy's Lemon Fig Preserves and Pecan Praline Figs. Two white, third-place ribbons for the Ginger Spiced Habanero Pears and Moonshine Vanilla Peach Jam were awarded. When the dust settled on Texas State Fairs, I had seven award winners. "You've got to be kidding" seemed like the most appropriate response to this news. Of course, next year came into clear view with hope and expectation for more blue ribbons.

Picklin' and Canning Up a Storm

In February, the world was aware of the dangers of the virus called corona. Our nation was in the middle of a very contentious presidential election. In March the country was virtually shut down, and people quarantined in their homes. During isolation, I began to pickle and can like I never had before. "Up a storm" would be a good idiom to describe my picklin' and canning. Because I like to keep busy and had time on my hands, I fired up the canning pot as the State Fair of Texas Creative Arts competition was announced to be going forward, though the 2020 State Fair of Texas was officially called off. The East Texas Fair simultaneously announced complete cancellation.

I entered several canned goodies and my spouse, Tammy, decided to join the State Fair competition fun. She submitted entries of her own. It only required a little arm-twisting to get her to compete. Competition was reported to be at an all-time high, so apparently, we were not the only ones resorting to isolation picklin' and canning.

By September 2020, we had the news that my Ginger-Spiced Habanero Pears and Garlic Pickled Okry had won blue ribbons at the State Fair of Texas. Tammy won a blue ribbon for her Aunt Rose's Marinated Mixed Veggies. She also won an Honorable Mention yellow ribbon for her Lemon Fig Preserves. I thank my great-grandmother Mamma Hacy — who had been gone for forty years — for the fig recipe. My rendition of Gran's (my Copeland grandmother's) Ol' Timey Pear Mincemeat won a second-place red ribbon, and the Pecan Praline Fig Preserves won an Honorable Mention yellow ribbon. That's six award winners at the 2020 State Fair of Texas. These winners brought our two-year total to nine items winning twelve ribbons—five blues, three reds, two whites and two yellows, but who's counting? Right!?!

A Cookbook Arises

In the middle of it all, the first *"Picklin' Parson Cookbook…Stories to Ponder When Uncle Sam's in a Pickle"* was published in November 2020. Prayerfully, it was hoped to be much more than a cookbook of recipes. Its primary purpose was to: 1) teach water bath canning, 2) share award-winning recipes, 3) spin stories to reflect on our

> *What good came out of COVID-19 isolation for you? What discoveries did you make about yourself, life matters, and global concerns during this challenging time?*

relationships and connections and ponder why we have so many divisions, 4) create new conversations that are respectful of others—even while challenging opinions, and 5) uplift the gift of being in loving, respectful relationships—no matter what.

Groups were formed around the cookbook via the new-to-me social communication of Zoom. A curriculum was designed to lead groups into new conversations for six to eight weeks. I formed a couple of groups that were fun, rich in conversation and certainly facilitated our getting to know—and greatly appreciate—one another. Some of my colleagues did the same with their congregations, friends and acquaintances, reading the book and using the curriculum. They reported similar positive results.

Before the groups concluded their time together, vaccines had arrived on the U.S. scene. People felt safer, so group members gathered in our home to make some apple butter. They also continued to ask tough questions about sociopolitical matters and divisions that made relationships in families tense and friendships frayed. Most importantly, we had a really good time engaging in wholesome conversations, getting to know one another better, respecting everyone, and above all else, loving each other as sisters and brothers.

2021 State Fairs of Texas and A Cookbook

In May I started pickling and canning for State Fairs with the hope of ribbons in mind. It's not that I am that competitive, but in an inexplicable kind of way, I have found

so much personal satisfaction from this agrarian art and sharing my joy and jars. I shared in my first cookbook that I once entered a heifer in the East Texas State Fair. She was the only one in her class and should have been a slam-dunk blue ribbon winner, but the judge liked two other heifers in a different class that he wanted to recognize and gave my calf an honorable mention. Think about it— the only one in the class, and you just get a "mention." How humiliating.

I hope my ribbon rhetoric is seen as a more playful celebration of "ribbon redemption" and plain old fun rather than braggadocios. I can still hear my daughter Emily laughing when I was sharing my ribbon success with my mom. Mom responded within earshot of my daughter, "Don't think because you won a few little ribbons that you are some sort of great cook." It was really kind of surprising and maybe the Parkinson's was speaking a bit, but Mom was quite uncharacteristically blunt. I can still hear Emily laughing out of control. To think of this scene makes me smile.

The 2021 Fair season started with the North Texas Fair and Rodeo in Denton, Texas. All my entries won a ribbon. Four of the entries won first-place blue ribbons: Bango Mango Chutney, Honey Apple Butter, Salty Dog Dills, and Triple-Play Pickled Garlic. Eight of the entries won second-place red ribbons: Blackberry Sage Chutney, Honey Onion Chutney, Mamma Hacy's Lemon Figs, MawMaw's Virginia Chunk Sweet Pickles, Spiced Peach Chutney, Ginger Tomato Chutney, and Strawberry Basil Jam. Five of the entries won third-place white ribbons: Amaretto Cherries, Blueberry Thyme Jelly, Minty Green Apple Chutney, Raspberry Mint Jam, and Garlic Pickled Okry.

The State Fair of Texas is always the most competitive of all the fairs. This year my daughter, Emily, and my wife, Tammy, joined in the competition. Emily and I went head-to-head on garlic scapes. She won a blue ribbon and the old man got a third place for his Triple-Play garlic scapes. My Honey Onion Chutney and Amaretto Cherries each won red ribbons for second place showings. This brought the three-year total State Fair of Texas winners to twelve. Tammy won a blue ribbon in 2020 for Aunt Rose's Marinated Mixed Veggies, Emily won with her garlic scapes in 2020. It has been so much fun.

Next was the West Texas Fair & Rodeo in Abilene, Texas. Nine of my eleven entries won ribbons and six of the ribbons were blue. "I can't believe this" seemed to be the most appropriate response. The blue-ribbon winners were: Honey Apple Butter, MawMaw's Virginia Sweet Chunks (pickles), Ol' Timey Pear Mincemeat, Strawberry Basil Jam, Triple-Play Garlic, and Blueberry Thyme Jam. The Blueberry Thyme Jam was a contender for best of show. The other three ribbon winners were all 2nd place red ribbons for: Amaretto Cherries, Honey Onion Chutney, and Ginger Tomato Chutney.

The East Texas State Fair in Tyler was the fair I grew up going to as a kid. Being on the fairgrounds brings back so many wonderful memories. The fair came with a very good result for my entrees. At the end of the day, nine of my fair entrees won blue ribbons, one red ribbon and six white ribbons came my way. What a surprise it was to see hanging by the Salty Dog Dills the coveted Triple Color Ribbon for the most points in the 2021 competition.

Thankful!!! For much more than ribbons!

From-the-Farm Gourmet
Pickles

/ˈpikəlz/

Optional
/ˈpitəlz/
(Claire Bear's pronunciation)

1. Small cucumbers preserved in vinegar, brine, or a similar solution.

2. Any fruits or vegetables preserved in vinegar or brine and used as a relish, chutney, chow chow, piccalilli, sauerkraut, etc.

3. Difficult or messy situations.

"We are in several pickles right now."

She Loves Her Some "Pituhls"

Our granddaughter, Claire Bear, is not yet four but since she was two, we knew that she loved her some pickles. As one still not pronouncing her "k's," she loves her some "pituhls." She loves her pickles just about anyway one can serve them up. She likes them dill, sweet, bread-and-butter style, and even spicy. It's not that the kid doesn't have a discerning palate. It is simply—as far as pickles are concerned—her taste buds are very desirous.

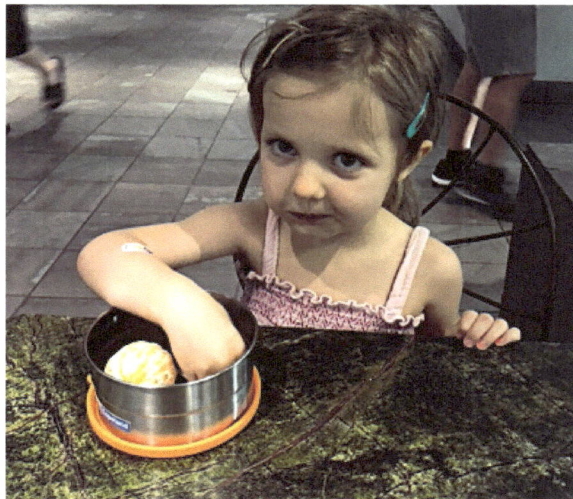

A Pickle Eatin' Kid

Claire Bear, an eighth-generation Texan, was the seventh generation to enjoy MawMaw's old-fashioned 12-day pickle recipe. When she tasted her first MawMaw Ellis sweet pickles at the age of two-and-a-half, she said, "Yummy. Ummmm. They my favit." Get this, her great-great-great-great-grandmother MawMaw Ellis would be proud. Then I asked myself, "How could MawMaw Ellis—who had rarely left the counties of Van Zandt and Henderson and never left the state of Texas—come up with a pickle recipe named after the state of Ol' Virginny?"

A little ancestry work revealed that MawMaw's great-grandparents were Robert and Jane Birdwell. They were both born in Virginia in 1751, twenty-five years before the Declaration of Independence. Could it be that this recipe was passed down from mothers to daughters all the way from a Virginia origin? If so, these Ol' Virginny treats are prepared according to a tenth-generation recipe. I like to think that as I belted out a laugh at Claire Bear's response "They my favit," her great-grandparents and their predecessors were also laughing from a heavenly perch.

New Recipes to Try Out

I eventually dilled a cucumber and made a "real" dill pickle. I called it a Kitchen Table Pickle, and it had onions and carrots in the mixture as well. The three pickles featured in this cookbook are some that Claire Bear has yet to try.

When I turn cucumbers into pickles, I typically use an old-fashioned style of brining that takes patience for the several day-process (see Appendix B). Figuratively speaking, the Creator cooked up the universe in six days and rested on the seventh. My seventh day of pickle-making has them coming out of the brine and going into the crisping phase. I don't rest from the process until Day Fourteen. There is something satisfying to me—a person who is normally driven with go-go-go as my mantra—about settling into a process that does not want to be rushed. It's good for my soul to make pickles the old-fashioned way.

We grew garlic on the farm for the first time in 2020/2021, and I was introduced to the garlic scape. It is the flower of the hard neck varieties of the garlic plants. When it appears and is ready to harvest, the garlic bulbs with their tasty cloves are three weeks from being mature.

The two scapes that we grew were German Hardy, which has a spiraling scape, and Elephant that produces a scape that is vertically straight with a marble-sized flower. They are delightfully tender and a milder, savory flavor of the clove coming to be. They make a beautiful jar of goodness. They can be found in some markets, and you can order them to be shipped in from larger garlic growers. We use all our scapes in our pickles and chutneys, with only a little left to sell to the public.

It is amazing to me how a common cucumber—a native of southern Asia but grown widely all over the world—can have such utility. From the cool addition to a salad to a pickled wonder with endless renditions, it is the vegetable that is directly associated with pickling and canning. We do know, however, that pickling is not limited to the cucumber; many vegetables or fruits can be easily pickled.

We have won State Fair blue ribbons for our pickled okra, pickled veggie medley, and pickled or spiced pears and peaches. Though we don't routinely grow cucumbers on the farm, many row crop farmers in our area do grow them and having them fresh in the summer can always be counted on.

Having trusted growers and farmers who produce their vegetables following "carefully grown" practices that we also follow is important to us. We want to offer delicious pickles that are good for you and always safe to consume. They will have our young ones saying "Yummy!" and their parents and grandparents smiling with delight.

Claire Bear loves her some Picklin' Parson pickles, and so will you. Her Pop, the Picklin' Parson, loves me some Claire Bear and Lily Billy too. Our youngest granddaughter,

Lily Grace—or Lily Billy to me—is an October 2020 born kid. Even at this tender age I can already tell that she is a pickle-eater in the making. I can't wait to hear her say, "Yummy!" or "They my favit!"—either one will do.

SALTY DOG DILLS

This is a rendition of the Kitchen Table Pickles featured in the first Picklin' Parson Cookbook. They are salty, spicy and spear-shaped. They also contain pickled carrots, sweet onions, garlic cloves, dill weed, red pepper pods, and garlic scapes. The pickles are quite attractive and delicious. Makes 12 pint jars.

Ingredients

- 6 pounds cucumbers
- 1 gallon water
- 2 ½ cups pickling salt
- 2 tablespoons pickle crisping granules
- 1 ½ gallons water
- 12 Carrots halved
- 8 cups Apple Cider Vinegar
- 2 tablespoons kosher salt
- 12 garlic cloves
- 12 garlic scapes
- 1 tablespoon dried dill seed
- ¼ cup mustard seeds
- ¼ cup coriander seeds
- 12 fresh dill weed heads
- 3 large, sweet onions, peeled and sliced into rings ¼-inch thick
- Retained garlic cloves or 12 new cloves
- 12 red pepper pods

Steps

1. On Day 1, cut about ¼ off the blossom end of the cucumber, and place the cucumbers in a crock.

2. Make a brine of a proportion of 2 ½ cups pickling salt to 1 gallon water in a large pot and bring to a boil. Pour the brine or salt water over the cucumbers in the crock while it is still boiling hot. Let stand for 7 days, daily skimming the foam that rises to the surface.

3. On Day 8, safely discard the brine. Place the whole pickles in a bath of ice water for 1 hour.

4. Cut the whole pickles into quarters or spears. Make a crisping solution with 2 tablespoons Pickle Fresh granules to 1 ½ gallons water in a large pot. Bring the

Pickle Fresh and water to a boil; pour the boiling crisping solution over the pickles that are in the crock. Let stand for 24 hours.

5. On Day 9, drain the crisping solution from the pickles. Rinse the pickles and place in ice cold water for 30 minutes.

6. Remove the tops of the carrots and slice in half; make sure the carrots are cut short enough to be under the solution with ½-inch headspace. Cut garlic cloves in half.

7. Place vinegar, salt, garlic, carrots, seeds, and dill heads in cook pot; bring to boil.

8. Place pickles in the hot, sterilized pint jars and half-fill the jars, retaining the remaining pickles. Fill the jars half-full of the hot liquid. Place two cloves of garlic, a red pepper pod, two carrot slices, a few onion rings, and a dill head in each jar. Put the remaining pickles in the jars and fill the jars with the hot liquid, leaving ½ inch of headspace. Make sure that the liquid completely covers the pickles that are just below the headspace. Wipe the inside of the rim with a damp paper towel.

9. Seal the jars with lids and bands. Place filled jars in boiling water canner for 15 minutes.

10. Transfer jars to a towel covering the surface to cool. After each jar has sealed, remove bands and wipe jars clean. When dry, screw the bands back to only lightly tight.

TRIPLE-PLAY PICKLED GARLIC

Perhaps the most meticulous preparation is this attractive jar of garlic. The German Hardy spiral scapes are seen on the outside of the jar. The Elephant garlic on the inside is packed vertically. The cloves of Kettle River garlic are in the center of the jar surrounded by the Elephant garlic and German Hardy scapes. Looks are one thing, but the savory, mild pickled taste is outstanding. Makes 12 pints.

Ingredients

- 2 pounds German Hardy garlic scapes
- 2 pounds Elephant garlic scapes
- 2 cups garlic cloves
- ¼ cup dill seed, one teaspoon per jar
- 3 tablespoons whole peppercorns
- 3 tablespoons whole coriander seed
- 2 tablespoons red pepper flakes
- 8 cups water
- 8 cups apple cider vinegar
- 1 cup pickling salt or kosher salt
- Fresh dill weed (optional as a garnish in the jars)

Steps

1. Trim each end of the German Hardy and Elephant garlic scapes, removing the pointy end beyond the bulb and trimming the tough bottom off the end.

2. Mix the dill seed, peppercorns, coriander seed, and red pepper flakes in a bowl and spoon out one tablespoon of the mixed spices per jar.

3. Start with a single German Hardy garlic scape and fit it horizontally into each hot, sterilized pint jar, following the curve of the jar. Repeat, using approximately 20 scapes per jar with just over ½ inch of headspace.

4. Cut a tube out of cardboard, plastic or thick paper, about 1 inch in diameter and place it in each jar. Put Elephant garlic scapes in each jar around the tube vertically, approximately 20 scapes. Fill the tube with garlic cloves, then remove the tube and finish stuffing garlic cloves in the center of the jar.

5. Mix water, cider vinegar and salt together in a pot, and bring to a boil. Stir to incorporate the salt.

6. Pour the hot vinegar brine over the garlic scapes in the pint jars, filling to within ½ inch of the top rim, covering all the garlic. Wipe the inside of the rim with a damp paper towel.

7. Seal the jars with lids and bands. Place filled jars in boiling water canner for 15 minutes.

8. Transfer jars to a towel covering the surface to cool. After each jar has sealed, remove bands and wipe jars clean. When dry, screw the bands back to only lightly tight.

Note: Wait at least two weeks for the flavors to infuse before eating. I find they're best at least six weeks later, so try to be patient.

CINNAMON STICK PICKLES

These are bright red pickle spears that are cinnamon and spice and everything nice. In color and flavor, they shout "happy" and "merry." They are spicy, but not extra hot. Thanksgiving and Christmas feasts should not be without these pickle treats. Have patience in making them; it involves three days of preparation. Makes 6 pints.

Ingredients

- 12 large cucumbers – peeled, seeded, and quartered lengthwise
- 1 cup pickling lime or calcium hydroxide
- 1 gallon water
- 1 gallon cold water, or as needed to cover
- 1 ¾ cups white vinegar, divided
- 1 ¼ cups water
- 12 ½ ounces cinnamon red hot candies
- 1 ½ teaspoons red natural food coloring
- ½ teaspoon alum
- 1 ¼ cups white sugar
- 4 cinnamon sticks – 4-inch

Steps

1. Put cucumber spears in a large container. Stir pickling lime into 1 gallon water in a large pitcher until the lime is dissolved; pour over the cucumbers. Refrigerate for 24 hours.

2. Drain cucumbers and rinse well; return to large container. Pour enough cold water over the drained cucumbers to cover. Soak at least 3 hours; drain. Transfer cucumbers to a large pot.

3. Stir 1 ¼ cup vinegar and 1 ¼ cup water together in a bowl; add cinnamon red hot candies. Set aside to soak, stirring occasionally.

4. Stir ½ cup vinegar, red food coloring, and alum together in a bowl until alum is dissolved; pour over the cucumbers. Put a lid on the pot, place the pot over medium heat, and bring the water to a boil. Reduce heat to low and simmer for 2 hours; drain and return cucumbers to the stockpot.

5. Pour cinnamon candy mixture that was set aside into a saucepan; add sugar and cinnamon sticks. Bring the mixture to a boil; cook and stir until the candies and sugar are dissolved completely into a syrupy liquid. Pour the liquid over the drained cucumbers in the stockpot. Refrigerate 8 hours to overnight.

6. Drain the liquid from the cucumbers, retaining it into a heavy saucepan; bring to a boil and pour again over the cucumbers. Refrigerate 24 hours.

7. Drain liquid again from the cucumbers into a heavy saucepan; bring to a boil and pour again over the cucumbers. Refrigerate another 24 hours.

8. Heat cucumbers and syrup to a boil. Pack cucumbers into the hot, sterilized jars, filling to within ½ inch of the top. Wipe the inside of the rim with a damp paper towel.

9. Seal the jars with lids and bands. Place filled jars in boiling water canner for 15 minutes.

10. Transfer jars to a towel covering the surface to cool. After each jar has sealed, remove bands and wipe jars clean. When dry, screw the bands back to only lightly tight.

Salty Dog Dill Pickles are the bomb! This East Texas Fair Triple Color Ribbon is evidence that judges agree.

Story Two

"Yes, It's Surely Enough!"

Few of us know the true meaning of the word "enough," at least in the way that she desired to understand it.

She was the quintessential Texas lady, one among the generation we call "great." To most who knew her, "saintly" comes to mind. She was a strong, well-educated, smart, articulate woman for sure, but she was a lady always in word and deed. Most everyone called Elizabeth Alexander Price "Ms. Elizabeth."

She was married to the love of her life, Richard "Dick" Price. He died before I came to pastor Lovers Lane United Methodist Church. Life jarred this faithful couple, as it has so many, with Dick's devasting diagnosis of Alzheimer's disease. I was told that the ten years before his death, she was right beside him—a constant presence when everything else was fleeting.

All I really knew about him was what church members would tell me about this man who was said to be as much a gentleman as Ms. Elizabeth was a lady. It was a better story when she would share about her beloved husband. She would close her eyes and a beautiful smile would appear on her glowing, gorgeous, nine-decades'-old face. She was set to take a trip back in time to the dance floor at the Adolphus Hotel in downtown Dallas. Dick would be twirling her around the dance floor in her mind's eye, but in my mind, the eye-catcher of any given evening on the town was this petite, energetic, breathtakingly beautiful woman.

When Dick died, she had some world traveling to catch up on and was off to interesting and exotic places. I got to accompany her on several of her trips. One of the things that inspired me about her was that she was always a learner. She loved to travel, mainly because she loved to learn. She loved to see beautiful sites and places that she had read about all her life. She especially loved seeing these sites with friends and loved learning in the midst of relationships. She wanted to get everything she could out of every day she was given.

Every day of an England trip Elizabeth wore high-heeled shoes and a classy, complimentary dress. There were no flats and no pant suits for her. On Sundays, just as it was back at home, a cute hat would top off her stylish outfits. When she packed, she put tissue paper between each garment. When she toured, she was at the head of the pack with her high heels clicking. They were no deterrent to walking for this ninety-year-old fireball.

Afternoon Tea and Chutney

I once went to afternoon tea at Harrods in London with her. Afternoon tea features scones, little sandwiches, and tiny cakes. High tea is in the late afternoon at 5 or 6 p.m. and is more substantial, I am told. High tea traditionally consisted of a meat dish, eggs, crumpets, potatoes, onion cakes, baked beans, or cheesy casseroles. The afternoon experience at Harrods was high-class, but definitely not high tea.

We were with a larger travel group from the church, but for the tea, it was just a few of us, mostly ladies. I was invited to sit at Elizabeth's table as her pastor—right beside her, as she instructed me where I was to reside for tea. We all had seats assigned by her, of course. This special high-tea treat was to cap off a wonderful England church heritage tour. It was fun, and she was in her element. Dressed to the nines, but not overly dressed for afternoon tea, she hosted us with elegant bossiness that caused us all to smile.

> *Have you ever been at a dinner where you felt out of your league? What were the circumstances? Ponder how you felt.*

Afternoon tea was a first for me, and let's just say I was out of my East Texas element where we made fun of tea sippers. Here I was in the "Neiman Marcusesque" Harrods, sipping tea with a table full of high-class ladies. I remember choosing a tea and hoping for the best. The Harrods' waiters made their way to our table with a three-tiered display tray/plate. It was intriguing to this parson who is a diehard meat eater but could suck it up for a real live tea party.

On the tray was an array of pastries and little sandwiches with no crust on the bread that my wife said were "finger sandwiches." Perhaps they call them finger sandwiches because it would take about ten of them to make a lunch. Not only was there no crust on the bread, but the sandwiches were smeared with something called clotted cream, and cucumbers took the place of the meat.

In East Texas, cucumbers only found their way to a sandwich by way of being a pickle. Accompanying these English cucumber sandwiches was a sweet, slightly spicy, veggie jelly of sorts called "chutney." It was very tasty. There were also some little pickled goodies that the English call piccalillis. Good news was that there was a little ham or prosciutto on one of the crustless wonders that also had a dab of what I was told was tomato chutney. It was delicious! Crustless mini sandwiches with ham and tomato chutney were the bomb for me; however, I only had two and made sure to nibble at them slowly with at least three bites.

Now, lest one should think I was freeing up my inner East Texas man, let me assure you, my "p's and q's" were well-minded. I was eating with the right table utensils and sipping my tea with the best of them. Ms. Elizabeth—well, she was in seventh heaven. The best part of this tea party was being with her and her guests. I did have to have a little parson fun with them toward the end of the event. I looked at her and said with a voice for the entire table to enjoy, "Elizabeth, do you think we can get a doggie bag for some of these treats we haven't eaten?" She rolled her eyes; my comment didn't even warrant a response. Everyone chuckled, but she stayed stoic. Inside I imagine she was happy that I was just being me— her fairly young parson who loved her very much.

Church Was a Holy Habit

She, along with her husband, Dick, were members of the church during the thirty-one years that Rev. Dr. Tom Shipp was pastor. He died suddenly at the age of fifty-eight in a finance meeting at the church, as details on the iconic windows of the sanctuary were being finalized.

Through her grief, Elizabeth had an idea for a pastor to follow Tom that she would share when the time was right. When she and Dick were members of the Methodist church in Highland Park, she was on a committee that

> **What "holy habits" do you admire and/or practice?**

brought a young man from East Texas named Don Benton to be an associate pastor. She and Dick always felt a connection with Don, and she suggested that he be considered for the senior pastor post to follow Tom. It happened just like she suggested.

This spirited lady loved all the Lovers Lane UMC pastors and was not shy to share her insights and critique. My predecessor Bill Bryan and I agreed that all of us benefited from her friendship and faithfulness. Bill and I could both share recollections of her pointed, pull-no-punches advice, but always shared in her kindness and love. She had a feel for what was best for the church, and she was one of the most beloved members of all time.

The last phone message I received from Elizabeth was after a sermon I preached on Christian family. It was a little "preachy" with some pointed directives. Someone told her about the sermon. She called and left this message on my voicemail: "Love, you really laid it on 'em this morning. Go get 'em, tiger." I really was not intending to "go get 'em," but if she liked it, after that call I strangely felt like growling.

She was in church nearly every Sunday from my first Sunday on April 5, 1998, and was set to turn ninety-seven years old a few days before she slipped away to feast at the heavenly banquet. She not only was in church the Sunday before her earthly departure, but she spoke in three services to dedicate the gift of a beautiful cross in the chancel of the sanctuary. She was such a conduit of God's love, but she told me many times about how overwhelmed she was with the acts of love shown to her by her "amazing church," as she put it. It was that belief that drove her the last months of her life.

Never Too Old to Learn

Elizabeth was such an integral part of our church and this parson's ministry. I hoped she would live forever, but life jarred her again with the diagnosis of pancreatic cancer that was inoperable and incurable. About two years before she succumbed to the pancreatic cancer that she bravely lived with for four years, she decided to take the Alpha course.

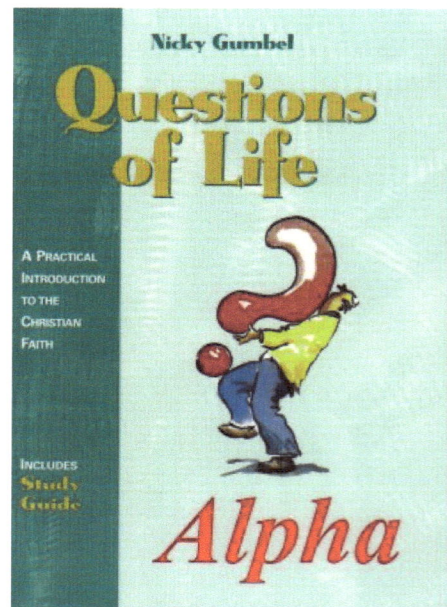

It is an eleven-week Christian short course that, at the time, about 1,000 of our members had taken. Eventually, eight thousand women and men who were incarcerated would experience with us the Alpha course. It is a two-hour weekly commitment to hear a lesson and then break into small groups for discussion. The class was at night, and her group was made up of mostly young adults. I asked her what she was doing taking that evening Alpha course, and she said, "Son, you're never too old to learn, and I drive just fine at night, thank you very much." She loved that course and the young people she came to know in her group.

Her group was very diverse—black and white, married and single, young and then there was Elizabeth. Two men in the group were a gay couple. I remember asking her about her group, and she said, "Son, I love them all. And God has taught me some things. He has changed my mind about some matters." I didn't push that comment, but I, along with others, witnessed her deepened faith and peaceful countenance that she attributed to her coursework with a group that had become very special to her.

When I just knew our time with her would be only weeks, I wanted to encourage her not to "Give up" was not in her vocabulary and certainly not in her heart. Not only did she never quit, but she didn't want us to quit either. At the time, I was writing a book about my mentor, Bill Hinson, whom she had met on a trip to the Passion Play in Oberammergau, Germany.

Bill and Elizabeth became fast friends. Knowing that she was ill and probably would not see the book published, I took the manuscript over to her and told her that I was dedicating the book to her: "To Elizabeth Price, who epitomizes the love of Lovers Lane." She thanked me, gave me a little kiss, and not only saw the book published in May 2006 but bought books for friends for the next two years. She wasn't finished; it wasn't enough. There was more that she had to do.

A Heart Full of Thanksgiving
In the last months of her life, she seemed to be driven by a purpose out of this world with a heart full of thanksgiving. Though she had given so much of herself to the church, she wanted to do more. She had commissioned some beautiful needlepoint kneelers that we enjoy today in Shipp Chapel.

Elizabeth talked to me one day about wanting the new chapel to have a beautiful cross. She said that she had seen one that she wanted me to see and give my opinion. So, one day I drove to her house in my Ford pickup that I made sure was clean and tidy for the tour. She was "dressed to the nines," but not as formal as she often was. Let's just say her outfit fit in my truck, and this 96-year-old battling aggressive cancer was striking. She looked like Mrs. Barkley on the old western *"The Big Valley."*

She took a first step onto the running board and settled in the passenger seat with a little help from yours truly. We went to see the cross that had caught her eye. It was at a Presbyterian Church where her younger sister was a member that was crafted by a local artist named Barvo Walker. I was very much attracted to this large and elegant altar cross. We then spent the day going from church to church, seeing crosses that she had identified. Then we talked to Barvo, who in two days gave us a sketch rendering of a cross that would take months to complete. Today, it is in Shipp Chapel and will bless us for years and years.

> *What have you been requested to do for another? What was the blessing in your response?*

It wasn't enough for her. Elizabeth wasn't finished. One day she called and said, "Son, our sanctuary needs a cross. Would you go over to Preston Hollow Presbyterian Church and see the gorgeous cross that is suspended in their sanctuary?" I said, "Elizabeth, what are you doing hanging out in all of these Presbyterian churches?" Slightly agitated she said, "I don't know, love. Maybe I'm predestined to do so. Just go see the cross, son."

I went to see the cross with a heart full of her, knowing our time with her here on earth was drawing nigh. After my latest cross-sighting, I called to tell her it was beautiful. My next call was to Barvo Walker. I told him that we needed a large cross for the sanctuary, like the one he had created for Preston Hollow. I also said, "Barvo, I don't think Elizabeth has many more weeks with us. The chapel is still under construction, and she will never see it finished. How long will it take to build the cross for the big room?" He said, "I'll get right on it ." Sure enough, he started immediately on a masterpiece for our stained-glass sanctuary, known as the largest stained-glass building in the United States.

In Elizabeth's last days—perhaps in part through Alpha and maybe even through her health challenge—she became really clear about the meaning of the cross. The cross became more and more beautiful to her, and she wanted us to have worship space that uplifted the cross.

During the thirty days that the sanctuary cross was being created, she slept a lot. I visited her on a Wednesday, and she said, "I am just going to rest in this bed until Sunday— except for bridge on Friday night. You know that a lady will get off her deathbed to get her hair done or play bridge." She was amazing.

The End and the Beginning

The beautiful cross was finished, and it was striking. It stands simple and magnificent, reflecting the many colors in the room. In the center, where the crossbars meet, it has a golden crown of thorns that reminds us that our Lord suffered on a cross for our redemption. On Sunday, August 21, 2008, Elizabeth got out of bed and put on one of her dozens of classic Sunday hats and her highest of heels, stepping into the Lovers Lane UMC pulpit for our 8:15, 9:30, and 11:00 worship services. She preached identically in each service without notes, saying, *"To the glory of God and in appreciation for the prayers and tangible expressions of loving support from the clergy, staff, and laity of Lovers Lane United Methodist Church."*

After the last presentation, I led her to the back of the chancel, and there were two young men there. Yes, they were the two gay men whom she loved and whom God used to "change her mind." One of the men said, "Pastor Stan, we're going to take her home. We'll take good care of her." She looked up at me and smiled and said, "Yes, they will, love. Get back in the sanctuary now. You have to preach, you know. I'll be fine with these wonderful young men taking care of me." One of her young friends carefully swept her little eighty-pound, 97-year-old body up in his arms, walked her to their waiting automobile, gingerly placed her in her seat, and took her home. They put her in bed and made sure that she was comfortable, and her caregivers were present. She died a few days later.

Before she passed over the Jordan, I visited Elizabeth one last time. She was in her bed and very weak. As lovingly as I could, I told her how blessed I was to call her friend; I also reminded her how many people loved her. Her last words to me in a hushed breath were "Son, I hope I have done enough." I prayed with her, and while praying, I could almost hear the Lord whispering in the ear of this saint, *"Elizabeth, it's enough. You've done plenty. Nothing has separated you from me. Nothing separates us now. You are home, and the heavenly banquet table is set. Your place is prepared for you among all your sisters and brothers."*

About that heavenly banquet, I have thought a lot about it lately, wondering if there will be those little crustless sandwiches with cucumber and chutney. It's fun to hope that there will be a few little amazing mini ham sandwiches with tomato chutney. It's satisfying to me to ponder. I too, have a thankful heart for one of the greatest ladies I have ever known. She lived through some jarring experiences, but she kept on giving. For this parson, Elizabeth put the "E" in "Enough."

This beautiful space will always be known for its iconic windows. Who could have guessed that the cross that Ms. Elizabeth envisioned would also be a centerpiece in this sanctuary?

From-the-Farm Gourmet
Chutneys
/ˈchətnēz/

1. A thick sauce of Indian origin that contains fruits, vinegar, sugar, and spices and is used as a condiment.

2. A delicious mush of fruit or vegetables of East Texas origin containing sweet Noonday onions, savory garlic, apple cider vinegar, light brown sugar, spices galore, and sometimes honey, pecans or tasty seeds that create a delightful crunch.

   Chef Andy Knudson really knows how to use chutney in his signature dishes.

Onions and Garlic Make Chutney

What is chutney for heaven's sake? Doesn't that sound like a question a Picklin' Parson might want answered? The answer is regarding the kind of chutney produced and sold under the Picklin' Parson label. First, let me say that Picklin' Parson chutney was born as a *From-the-Farm Gourmet* delicious creation.

From-the-Farm Gourmet is a concept with the purpose of bringing fresh produce that is carefully or organically grown directly from the farm to tables in homes. There is an increasing desire to know where our produce comes from. Our Stillwater Farm produce is grown with very low or no chemicals. Cultivation and harvesting follows safe eco-friendly farming practices that are valued today, especially by younger and health-conscious consumers.

Our *From-the-Farm Gourmet* chutney is a spicy, savory condiment. Its robust flavor comes from fruit, vegetables, herbs, apple cider vinegar, brown sugar, natural honey, and an array of spices, as well as sweet onions and garlic—both grown on the farm.

Chutney balances a variety of dishes; glazes any meat, chicken, or fish; jazzes up a cheese appetizer; couples with sour cream for a delightful dip; and simply spreads on a cracker to tingle the taste buds. From-the-Farm Gourmet Chutney can turn a cheeseburger into an extraordinary meal, make a grilled cheese sandwich come alive with flavor, and complement a Monte Cristo, making a French chef say Oh là là!

Sweet Onions and Savory Garlic

For the better part of the last decade, we have grown literally tons of Noonday onions. This onion is a yellow granex variety originating in Texas. The most famous version of the yellow granex onion is grown in South Georgia and branded the "Vidalia."

The specific variety of onion is the most important factor in determining taste, flavor, and sweetness, but so is the soil in which the onion is grown. The soil in Noonday, Texas — close to Tyler — is sandy loam above a red clay base. The sand allows for maximum expansion of the bulb in the sand. This East Texas soil is also just the right blend of acidic and alkaline elements to peak the sugar content, making it the sweetest onion in the world. "No sulfur" is an important dynamic in growing and making onions sweet.

Another very good thing is that hardly any insects and no deer or wild hogs mess with onions and garlic. Whether from South Georgia or East Texas, these onions put the "s" in sweetest.

In 2020 we began to grow garlic in a big way. We have had success with primarily three varieties of garlic on the farm—German Hardy, Kettle River Giant, and Elephant. Our garlic is grown with organic practices, and it has a fantastic consistency and flavor. The Elephant and the German Hardy also produce a green scape along with the clove. The scapes have a milder garlic flavor contained in the freshness of a green shoot that flowers.

Chefs all over the world keep an eye out for the scape harvest, which is three to four weeks before the bulbs are fully mature. The garlic cloves give rise to one of the most pungent and unique flavors on earth.

Savory with a Sweet Finish and Spiced with a Light Crunch

Our chutneys comes in two basic groupings; one is defined as "savory" and the other as "spiced." Some say they taste like the seasons—spring-to-summer and autumn-to-winter—but be assured any of our chutneys are delicious in all seasons and beautiful to boot.

Savory chutney complements the main ingredients of fruit, vegetables and onion with herbs and the sweetness of a brown-sugar or honey finish. Spicy chutney complements the chunky fruit and onions in every jar with crunchy apples, candied pecans, and seeds. Whatever the season and no matter the occasion, chutney brings the farm to the table.

If you consider yourself a stranger to chutney, consider yourself introduced and encouraged to visit us online at www.picklinparson.com or stillwatermarket.farm. Become even more familiar with this eye-pleasing, wonderfully tasty chutney by buying one, two, or all six of the unique flavors. You'll find that chutney is the food version of "life of the party," and on a calmer note, it will liven up any basic meal. The colorful charm in a jar of chutney is only superseded by the lip-smacking flavor of its dollop of delight.

We farm to gladly bring onions and garlic, peaches, and pecans to your kitchen table. When the produce comes to the table by way of handsomely jarred and packaged savory and spiced chutney, let yourself smile with anticipation.

When you see the Picklin' Parson label, think of *From-the-Farm Gourmet* and "award-winning." Best of all, know that delicious is our goal, enhancing food flavor is our aim, and we are always "pickling with a purpose." Our 2021 chutneys are:

Honey Onion	(Gold)
Ginger Tomato	(Red)
Sage Blackberry	(Purple)
Bango Mango	(Yellow)
Spiced Peach	(Orange)
Minty Green Apple	(Green)

GINGER TOMATO CHUTNEY

Ginger Tomato (red) features never refrigerated, red-to-the-core, vine-ripe tomatoes and golden, sun-kissed raisins. The soft red color paints the perfect blend of ginger, pepper, cumin, and lime. Savory with a lightly sweet finish says it all. Heavenly! Makes 12 pints.

Ingredients

- 8 cups tomatoes, peeled, cored, and medium-diced, from approximately 4 pounds of tomatoes
- ¼ cup minced garlic
- 6 cups chopped sweet onions
- 2 cups golden raisins, currants, craisins or any combination
- 1 cup garlic scapes, green onion tops, or mild green pepper
- 2 cups brown sugar
- 2 tablespoons pickling salt
- 1 lime, juiced and scraped for zest
- 1 tablespoon powdered ginger
- 1 tablespoon chili pepper flakes, more if desired
- 1 teaspoon ground cumin
- 1 tablespoon12 black pepper
- 1 ½ cups apple cider vinegar
- 2/3 cup Clear Jel or 2 boxes low or no-sugar pectin

Steps

1. Bring a stockpot of water to a boil. Add tomatoes; submerge in boiling water for 1 minute, and then put them in ice cold water in a bowl. Peels will easily come off. Cut the tomatoes into pieces.

2. Add prepared onions, garlic, salt, pepper, cumin, ginger, lime zest, red pepper flakes and oil to a stockpot, and cook for five minutes.

3. Combine tomatoes and remaining ingredients in a stockpot. Bring to a boil, then reduce to a simmer. Tip: Put 2/3 cup apple cider vinegar in a shaker jar and add the Clear Jel to the mixture. Shake until it is a white liquid, then add to the heating mixture.

4. Cook up to 90 minutes or until the tomato mixture is slightly thickened, stirring often to prevent scorching. Add salt or other seasoning to taste.

5. Ladle hot chutney into hot, sterilized pint jars, leaving ½ inch headspace. Wipe the inside of the rim with a wet paper towel.

6. Seal the jars with lids and bands to finger-tight, not snug. Place jars in boiling water canner for 15 minutes.

7. Transfer jars to a towel covering the surface to cool. After each jar has sealed, remove bands and wipe jars clean. Towel dry the lids, jar threads and band threads. When dry, screw the bands back on the jars to lightly tight.

RED FISH or SNAPPER ON THE HALF SHELL
with
GINGER TOMATO CHUTNEY
from Chef Andy Knudson

In Texas there is a lot of Gulf of Mexico sport fishing and many people cook their fish on the "Half Shell." My interpretation of "half shell" is that you take the filet and grill it whole. When I grill Red Fish or Snapper I leave the scales on the fish so it does not stick to my grill.

Recipe

2 (each side) of Red Snapper, Grouper, or Redfish
1 jar of Picklin' Parson Tomato Ginger Chutney
2 large metal spatulas for taking fish off grill

Season your fish with salt and pepper, or whatever spice blend that you prefer. Let this marinate over night, or at least for a couple of hours. Get your grill hot and ready, it should be about 375 to 400 degrees. Place the skin side down and cook for about 10 to 15 minutes depending on the thickness of the filets.

Once the fish is cooked to your satisfaction remove the filets and place them in a bowl shaped out of foil, and cover with the tomato chutney. Close the top of the foil over the bowl and let it sit for 5 minutes so it gets all that flavor. Best served with rice and grilled vegetables!

HONEY ONION CHUTNEY

Honey Onion (gold) is our most popular and our only recipe with real wildflower honey complementing the sweetness of the onion. It is golden in color and sprinkled with red and yellow pepper flakes. It pops with the natural flavors of ground mustard seeds and minced garlic. The best!. Makes 10 pints.

Ingredients

- 8 cups sweet onion slices (prefer 9 or 10 pounds Noonday or Vidalia onions that should yield 8 cups of onion slices, mandolin-sliced is best)
- ½ cup garlic scapes cut like chive chips (green onion tops or sweet green peppers can be substituted)
- 2 cups apple juice
- 1 cup apple cider vinegar
- ¼ cup fresh minced garlic
- 1 tablespoon salt
- 1 teaspoon black pepper
- 1 teaspoon ground mustard
- 1 tablespoon crushed red pepper flakes
- 2/3 cup Clear Jel or 2 boxes low or no-sugar pectin
- 1 tablespoon butter to reduce foaming
- 2 cups honey
- ¾ cup light brown sugar

Steps

1. Cut and peel onions; slice in half and cut each in half again. Cut into ¼-inch slices widthwise. A mandolin slicer can be used, but always use this helpful utensil with extra caution. The onions will cook down more like string slices than chunks.

2. Add prepared onions, apple juice, apple cider vinegar, garlic, salt, pepper, mustard, and red pepper flakes to a stockpot. Gradually stir in Clear Jel or pectin. Add butter to reduce foaming.

3. Bring to a boil that can't be stirred down over high heat, stirring constantly.

4. Add the honey and brown sugar; return to a full boil and let boil for 1 minute, stirring constantly. Remove from heat; skim foam if needed.

5. Ladle hot chutney into hot, sterilized pint jars, leaving ½ inch headspace. Wipe the inside of the rim with a wet paper towel.

6. Seal the jars with lids and bands to finger-tight, not snug. Place jars in boiling water canner for 15 minutes.

7. Transfer jars to a towel covering the surface to cool. After each jar has sealed, remove bands and wipe jars clean. Towel dry the lids, jar threads and band threads. When dry, screw the bands back on the jars to lightly tight.

CRACKED PEPPER CHICKEN SALAD
with
HONEY ONION CHUTNEY
from Stillwater Farm Market Store

At the Stillwater Farm Market Store, we make our chicken salad with chicken breast meat that is grilled to tender and then pulled into pieces and shreds. Mayonnaise is added and chopped celery, along with a sprinkling of red onions, with a good portion of cracked black pepper. Spread the bread slices with the Honey Onion Chutney for a delicious sandwich.

SAGE BLACKBERRY CHUTNEY

Sage Blackberry (purple) highlights the sweet taste of blackberries in a smooth, seedless pulp with sweet onion strings and the earthy, peppery taste of sage. The usual response to this boldly colorful, scrumptious spread is "Amazing!" Makes 12 pints.

Ingredients

- 8 cups seedless juice from 1 gallon of blackberries
- 15 to 20 sage leaves
- 1 tablespoon dried sage
- 10 cups sliced sweet onions (start with 12 pounds raw sweet onions)
- 2 cups apple juice
- 1 cup apple cider vinegar
- 2 tablespoons fresh minced garlic
- ½ cup garlic scapes cut like chives or green onion tops
- 2 teaspoons salt
- 1 teaspoon black pepper
- ½ teaspoon ground mustard
- 1 tablespoon crushed red pepper flakes (add more if heat is preferred)
- 2 tablespoons of pecan or vegetable oil
- 5 ½ cups sugar
- ½ cup Clear Jel or 2 boxes low or no-sugar pectin
- 1 tablespoon butter to reduce foaming (I always use it.)

Steps

- Wash blackberries and add them to a stockpot. Bring to a boil, while mashing them with a potato masher.

- Take the syrupy liquid and put in a blender 3 or 4 cups at a time and blend.

- Strain the liquid to separate it from the seeds and thicker pulp. Mash the mixture with a spoon to get the juice to flow into an 8-cup measuring bowl under the strainer. Discard the strained seed and pulp.

- Cut and peel onions; slice in half and cut each in half again. Cut into ¼-inch slices widthwise. A mandolin slicer can be used, but always use this helpful utensil with extra caution. The onions will cook down more like string slices than chunks.

- Add prepared onions, apple juice, vinegar, garlic, salt, pepper, mustard, red pepper flakes sage leaves and dry sage and oil to a stockpot, and cook for five minutes.

- Add berry juice and sugar to the onions. Heat and gradually stir in Clear Jel; then add butter. Bring to a boil that can't be stirred down over high heat, stirring constantly.

- Ladle hot chutney into hot, sterilized pint jars, leaving ½ inch headspace. Wipe the inside of the rim with a wet paper towel.

- Seal the jars with lids and bands to finger-tight, not snug. Place jars in boiling water canner for 15 minutes.

- Transfer jars to a towel covering the surface to cool. After each jar has sealed, remove bands and wipe jars clean. Towel dry the lids, jar threads and band threads. When dry, screw the bands back on the jars to lightly tight.

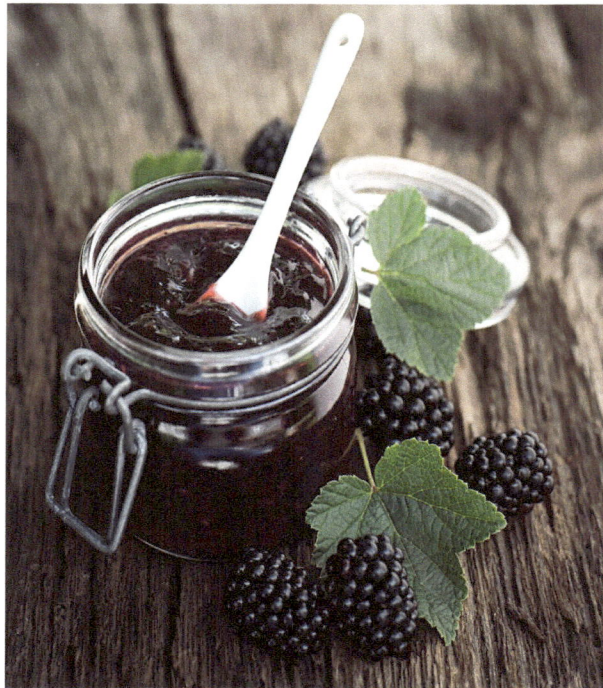

PIMENTO CHEESEBURGER
with
SAGE BLACKBERRY CHUTNEY
from Stillwater Farm Market Store

Talk about colorful, beautiful, and delicious, try this combination. In the Stillwater Farm Market Store, our recipe for pimento cheese starts with an equal amount of cheddar and mozzarella cheese. Add real mayonnaise and sprinkle with bright red pimentos and tangy capers to top it off. Make a hamburger patty the way you like it. Toast a good bun, spread with pimento cheese, and top the meat off with a dollop of Sage Blackberry Chutney. Woo-hoo!

Friendship and support, like what I have had from the very creative Mark Holubec, is a true gift. The Picklin' Parson logo, labeling, this chutney display and more was Mark's creation.

Story Three

"You Matter! Wannaknowwhy?"

Sometimes I hear talk of a present-day civil war in our country from people who don't have a clue about what they speak.

Peter Weato and my many friends who have come our way from Liberia know the horrors of such a war and the deadly realities. Arguably, no story changed our church and this parson's ministry more than the story of Peter Weato and his wonderful family.

In the year 2000, Lovers Lane UMC embarked on a major marketing project to share stories from members. I had been in Dallas for a couple of years, but I was becoming increasingly aware of the power of the stories in our midst. I, along with others, believed that the inspiration of stories could make a positive impact on Dallas and the larger world.

Wannaknowwhy.com

Not only did we have the stories, but we also had the professional marketing talent in people who were willing to give their time and energy to make the venture happen. Our efforts quickly had an inspired name—Wannaknowwhy—and a website, wannaknowwhy.com. Ours is a very diverse and multicultural congregation. The message of radical acceptance of all was our intended statement to the larger world, the purpose being to attract all kinds of people to our fellowship that for years heralded a nonqualified statement: "YOU are welcome."

A couple of members led the charge and a few others made generous contributions to fund this marketing initiative featuring television and radio spots, billboards on strategic thoroughfares, and newspaper and magazine ads, along with the growing dynamic of the internet.

The domain wannaknowwhy.com was meant to be intriguing with tag lines in bright yellow script with a professional black background and striking black and white photos. It was innovative and had the city stirring about "Who are the wannaknowwhy people?"

Going to the wannaknowwhy.com site and clicking on the face of the featured storyteller would reveal their unique sagas. The tag lines in ads and on strategically placed billboards were:

- You're loved just the way you are.
- Joy is possible.
- Your life has meaning.
- You can change the world.
- You can find your sanctuary in ours.
- You matter.

It worked! We had a billboard of a young deaf woman with the tag, "You Make a difference " wannaknowwhy? Deaf people read her story and came with their families and friends like never before. We told a story of a young man with severe physical disfigurement, as well as others with disabilities, around the tag "Your life has meaning" wannaknowwhy? Persons with all kinds of special needs started showing up, and many were and youth with their families.

A doctor, who was gay, and a longtime member told his story of rejection from churches since his youth. His tag was "You're loved just the way you are" wannaknowwhy? This message resonated with the LGBTQ community, and "they" became "us," testing the welcome. It must have passed, given the number of people who came into the fellowship.

Following the posting of Peter Weato's story, not only did Liberians migrate our way, but African people from twenty different countries started making their way to Lovers Lane UMC. In a matter of months, we began to see our North Dallas church—tucked into one of the most affluent and white neighborhoods in Dallas—become the place many Africans were now calling HOME. Peter's striking photo and the straightforward statement he made touched many hearts.

You Matter—wannaknowwhy?

My story begins as Liberia, West Africa was in the middle of civil war. Atrocities were being perpetrated on people by the government. Horrible brutality including flogging, persistent rapes, summary executions, castrations and dismemberments were a part of life from the early 1990s until recently.

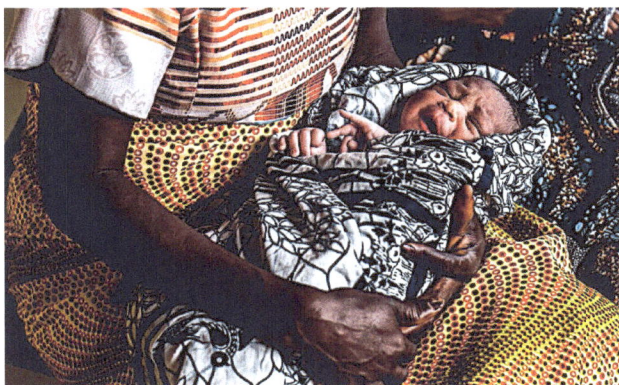

I was shot by drunken soldiers on a killing spree outside the John F. Kennedy Hospital in Liberia. The soldiers, thinking I was dead, threw me in the back of a dump truck with other bodies of my tribesmen who had been executed moments before. They dumped me in the heap of bodies on the beach of my homeland between the water and the bush. As night fell, I crawled to the bush and then into town where I spent the night in a dumpster outside the Nigerian Embassy. At dawn, I made my way back to my house to discover that it was burned to the ground, and my wife Betty and our five children were missing. I fled to the Ivory Coast, and at the American Embassy I found refuge. But my family was presumed to be dead.

In September 1993 in Dallas, Texas I started to rebuild my life. After three years of separation, I heard the miraculous news that my wife Betty and my children Emmanuel, Nancy, Peter Jr., Peterian, and Mehn were alive and in a refugee camp on the Ivory Coast. Our baby had died on the difficult trip from Monrovia to Zoe Geh. I immediately began the process to reunite with them here in Dallas. After some months, the process was complete; the reunion was one of the sweetest moments of my life.

Another important day was May 26, 1996, when my family and I became members of Lovers Lane United Methodist Church. We were looking for a church where we could worship. We wanted to find a congregation that would open its arms to us with acceptance and with the love of Christ that we so desperately needed after all the trauma we had experienced. Our church has been there for us since the first day we stepped inside the sanctuary. I have said before that we found our refuge in the United States but our sanctuary—safe haven—we found in the sanctuary of the congregation so rightly named—Lovers Lane—as we discovered there a love that was real. Lovers Lane UMC made us understand that we mattered to them and to God.

Not only was Peter's story read in the greater Dallas area, but a Liberian soldier read it in Monrovia. This colonel had been in a place of authority and had ordered the shooting of Peter and hundreds of others from the Gio tribe. The colonel read the story via the internet all the way across the Atlantic. He testified to being so happy and grateful that one person thought to have been slaughtered among the masses had survived the massacre on that horrible day.

The colonel immediately went to St. Paul Lutheran Church in Monrovia. During the civil war in that infamous time of massacre, bodies were stacked like cordwood and blood coated the floor of the desecrated church. The colonel confessed to the pastor there, professed his faith in a Jesus whose forgiveness was offered freely. He then was baptized.

> **When have you witnessed graciousness and forgiveness shared that made a difference?**

Soon afterward Peter and the colonel met and became friends. Even when the colonel was diagnosed with cancer the two continued to meet. They visited regularly until the colonel died. Because of Peter's graciousness and amazing forgiveness, the former foe died with a degree of peace that had escaped him for nearly two decades.

Nothing "Civil" About Civil War

Peter is a Gio tribesman, a scapegoated people largely blamed by the government for the insurrection of the 1990s led by Prince Yormie Johnson. Senator Prince Johnson's rebel warriors and the coup cause was initiated from this part of the country, Nimba County.

Senator Johnson was a former rebel leader—and to some degree a folk hero—due to his prominent role in the civil war. His escapades were remarkable, but no story made more of an impression than the one in which he captured President Samuel Doe, and the gruesome scene that followed.

President Doe himself had led a coup d'état and had overthrown and murdered the previous president William Tolbert Jr. President Doe, in Johnson's custody, was front and center in the videotaped spectacle that was broadcast around the world. Johnson—while sipping a Budweiser beer and being fanned by an assistant—had his men cut off Doe's ears and do other unspeakable, torturous acts before killing him. Upon my first trip to Liberia, Peter introduced me to Prince Johnson as we met in the Senator's office in Monrovia.

There was little that is "civil" about the civil war in Liberia in the 1990s. It was brutal and horrific; innocent citizens—like Peter and Betty Weato and their family—got caught up in the jarring throes of its evil. This parson believes that God specializes in redeeming for good the most jarring of life circumstances. The atrocities of Liberia's war brought the Weatos to Dallas and into our faith family, but that was only the beginning of the story.

Peter had come into my office in 2010 and shared a dream of having a hospital in his home region of Zoe Geh. Peter and I prayed about his dream. Shortly after the meeting, I introduced Peter to a doctor and his wife—Susan and Woody Gandy. The Gandys were moved by Peter's dream, his passion and determination. They had the means and the incredible generosity to make a difference. They helped fund the endeavor, and construction on this 100-plus bed medical center was quickly underway.

A Life-Changing Hospital Visit

I went to Zoe Geh, Nimba County, Liberia to witness for myself the hospital and the work of the doctors, nurses and staff who served there. Lovers Lane UMC also had partially funded the project, purchased an ambulance, helped construct a maternity ward and assisted with other construction.

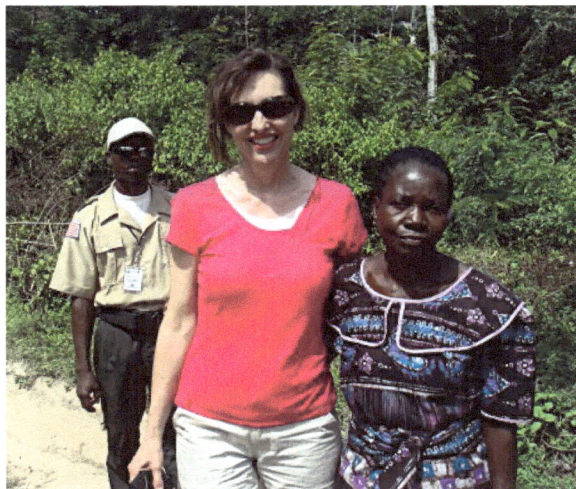

The first time I went to see the Zoe Geh Medical Center was in 2012. I was blessed to go and see the hospital and meet the people served there. We made a difficult two-day journey to the far outreaches of the country on the border of the Ivory Coast and Liberia. In this little underserved area of Liberia there is a township called Zoe Geh. Seeing a white face in the bush of Liberia was not a regular occurrence to those in such a remote area. Peter and his friends were trying to prepare me for what was coming.

When we drove up, there were people who had been waiting for days; some had walked from Côte d'Ivoire or the Ivory Coast. There was a celebration of singing and dancing; branches were waved as the crowd gathered around us. There were hundreds of people who had walked through the bush—some for days—to be there. We got out of the vehicles and entered the hospital where we saw people being treated for malaria and a mother with triplets, one of which was dying. There were others who had various sicknesses and diseases.

As we walked out of the hospital there were reporters getting quotes and a throng of people accompanying us. I asked what they were singing, and Peter said, "They are singing praises to God for bringing you to their village." The celebration went on for hours. Humbled and not knowing quite what to do with this radical hospitality, I began to interact with newfound sisters and brothers.

I was overwhelmed by a sense of unending gratitude. Different groups of people from all the surrounding villages brought gifts of chickens, goats, and rice, laying them at our feet. It felt like true undeserved grace was being given to me. I was thankful for the Weatos, who had the vision of the hospital. I was grateful for Susan and Woody who were the first to embrace the Weatos' vision. I was appreciative of our parishioners who were moved to give to this lifesaving work. I was so appreciative for the hard work of the people living in Zoe Geh to start this hospital.

A Jarring Tragedy

The cheering had carried on for hours, but it stopped that day when we got jarring news that a big truck carrying bananas that was also loaded with people had crashed. We had seen that very truck and the people atop the bananas just hours before in the town a few miles from the hospital. The overloaded truck failed to climb a hill and had rolled back down the hill out of control. The horrific accident left two dead at the scene; one would die en route to the hospital. At the hospital I saw some of the most horrific wounds I had ever seen—broken bones and lacerations. The words I choose to pen cannot come close to describing what I saw with my eyes.

The doctors and nurses and Peter worked all night with the wounded. One young man had to be told that his wife was among the dead. I was told that they had five children. He was devastated and had to be held up as he wept uncontrollably. It was as difficult a scene as I have ever witnessed. I felt so helpless. I couldn't even talk to the man and do the caring parson work because I didn't speak his tribal language.

Then Peter came on the scene. He hugged the man close. Then he whispered in his ear in a voice that I could hear and understand. Peter said to the broken man, "God loves you and God knows your pain." Then he spoke in his tribal language. He continued in English, "God holds your wife in his arms right now and wants to send you comfort and give you a peace. You may not know how you will cope, how you will tell your children and her parents. You may not know how you are going to care for your family by yourself, but God will help you make a way." He and the man then talked to each other in their native language. It was surreal, one of the most touching moments I had ever witnessed.

I have always carried with me that scene of tragedy and words of hope that Peter shared with a devasted husband and father. We would leave Zoe Geh for Monrovia. The fanfare was gone, but the friendly waves of "goodbyes" were genuine. I joked to Peter when they found out the white man was just a human being like them, it was not quite as exciting.

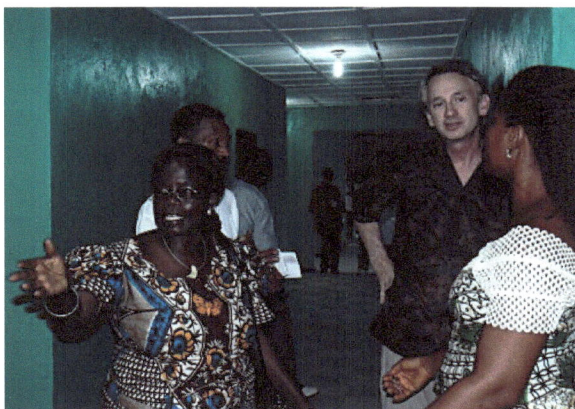

Mango Season in Liberia

As we drove out of Zoe Geh through the town where the banana truck of the tragedy was parked just days before, there was a similar scene. It was a smaller truck in town with a green fruit and several people atop the load. The fruit on the truck was recognizable as mangoes. The Liberians call them plums.

Mango or plum season in Liberia starts in the late dry season and extends to the early rainy season, so usually sometime in March through May-June. There seem to be two distinct varieties in Liberia. There are early-season mangoes which are long and skinny and when ripe, just start to shade to yellow. The late-season mangoes are more like what you see in stores in the U.S.—shorter, fat, and with a red cast to them when ripe.

This story ends with more chutney on the kitchen table. This section begins what I call spiced chutney, and it features mangoes and other fruit among sweet onions and lots of delicious spices. This chutney recipe I dedicate to Peter and Betty and the beloved people of Zoe Geh, to symbolize our coming together and the transforming of jarring life experiences into sacred living. I have sprinkled into the chutney what I call Bango Mango—black nigella or black cumin seeds and white sesame seeds.

The picklin' and canning of the ebony and ivory seeds among the happy yellow mango chutney takes this parson to a thankful place. I hope it will do so for you and others too.

Wanna know why there's a Zoe Geh Medical Center? Because people saw a need, joined hands and hearts, and made it happen.

BANGO MANGO CHUTNEY

In honor of Betty and Peter Weato and Susan and Woody Gandy, Bango Mango was created. Bango Mango (yellow)—popping with spices, an occasional crunch of pink peppercorn, and a bit of heat—is convincing that it is more than just a looker, though its spectacular natural color is remarkable. This colorful goodness in a jar was inspired by the friendship of a dear Liberian family as revealed in the delightful mixture of black nigella or black cumin seeds and white sesame seeds. Tasty! Makes 10 pints.

Ingredients

- 6 cups mango chunk
- 2 cups sliced sweet onions
- 4 serrano peppers
- 2 tablespoons pecan oil (or olive oil or vegetable oil)
- 1 tablespoon ground ginger
- 1 tablespoon chopped or minced garlic
- 1 cup golden raisins
- 2 cups white vinegar
- 2 cups granulated sugar
- 1 tablespoon red pepper flakes
- 2 teaspoons whole pink peppercorns
- 2 teaspoons whole black nigella seeds
- 2 teaspoons ground coriander
- 2 teaspoons kosher salt
- 1 teaspoon ground cumin
- 1 teaspoon turmeric
- 1 teaspoon saffron (optional)
- 1 tablespoon of Nigilia seeds
- 1 tablespoon of Seseme seeds
- ½ cup Clear Jel or 2 boxes low or no sugar needed pectin

Steps

1. Peel the mangoes, slice, and chunk. Medium ripe mangoes are best. Put them in a bowl.

2. Cut and peel onions; slice in half and cut each in half again. Cut into ¼-inch slices widthwise. A mandolin slicer can be used, but always use this helpful utensil with extra caution. The onions will cook down more like string slices than chunks.

3. Cut serrano peppers into pieces. Retain as many seeds as desired; the heat will be determined largely by the seeds that are added.

4. Heat the oil over medium-high in a medium stock pot. Add onions and peppers and sauté in the ginger and garlic for 5 minutes. Add raisins, vinegar, sugar, spices and seeds; bring to a boil, stirring constantly.

5. At the first sign of boiling of the mixture, add the mangoes. Add the Clear Gel and stir all the ingredients into a beautiful yellow mixture.

6. Bring it to a rapid boil and reduce heat to medium-low. Steady simmer for 15 minutes; be careful not to overcook the mangoes. The chutney still should be lumpy.

7. Ladle hot chutney into hot, sterilized pint jars, leaving ½ inch headspace. Wipe the inside of the rim with a wet paper towel.

8. Seal the jars with lids and bands to finger-tight, not snug. Place jars in boiling water canner for 15 minutes.

9. Transfer jars to a towel covering the surface to cool. After each jar has sealed, remove bands and wipe jars clean. Towel dry the lids, jar threads and band threads. When dry, screw the bands back on the jars to lightly tight.

CHEESY GRILLED CHEESE
with
BANGO MANGO CHUTNEY

Take a couple buttered slices of artisan bread; spread one side of each piece of bread with Bango Mango chutney. Add your favorite cheese combination. You can bake the sandwich, or cook it in a skillet until it is golden brown. This is not your mama's grilled cheese sandwich, the spicy, fruity chutney is the proof. Served with a bit of tomato soup, tops off a true sandwich delicacy.

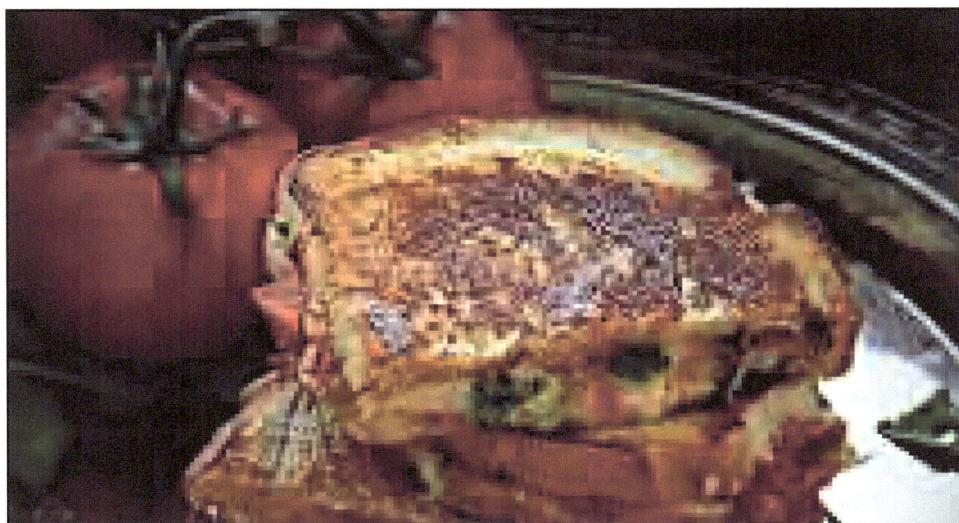

SPICED PEACH CHUTNEY

Spiced Peach (orange) blends textures, colors, and flavors of golden raisins, red craisins, Granny Smith apples, sweet onions, cinnamon candied pecans, and the juice of limes—making any mouth water with anticipation. The spices are purely autumn with cinnamon, nutmeg, and turmeric. Delightful! Makes 12 pints.

Ingredients

- 8 cups (8 pounds) peaches, cut into chunks
- 3 cups sweet onions, thinly sliced (a mandolin slicer may be used)
- 1 tablespoon cinnamon
- 1 tablespoon ground turmeric
- 1 tablespoon nutmeg
- 2 tablespoons minced garlic
- 4 tablespoons pecan oil (olive oil can be substituted)
- 4 cups apple cider vinegar
- 1 cup golden raisins
- 1 cup red craisins
- 1 cup black raisins
- 2 cups granulated sugar
- 2 cups light brown sugar
- ½ cup fresh lime juice (about 2 limes)
- ½ cup Clear Jel or 2 boxes low or no-sugar needed pectin
- 1 tablespoon kosher salt
- 2 cups chopped, toasted candied praline pecans
- ¼ cup brandy

Steps

1. Peel peaches, remove the stone/seed and slice; keep them in a bowl. (Peaches can be submerged in boiling water for 1 minute and then put in ice cold water; the peeling will easily come off. Cut in half and remove the stone/seed.)

2. Cut and peel onions; slice in half and cut each in half again. Cut into ¼-inch slices widthwise. A mandolin slicer can be used, but always use this helpful utensil with extra caution. The onions will cook down more like string slices than chunks.

3. Sauté the onions, cinnamon, turmeric, nutmeg, and garlic in the oil in a stockpot over medium heat for 5 minutes.

4. Stir in the peaches, vinegar, raisins, sugar, and lime juice. Cook, stirring occasionally, until sugar dissolves. Stir in the Clear Jel.

5. Bring to a boil, reduce heat and simmer, stirring occasionally, 20 minutes or until thickened. (Do not overcook, there should be peach lumps in the mixture.)

6. Add the pecans and brandy and stir for 1 minute.

7. Ladle hot chutney into hot, sterilized pint jars, leaving ½ inch headspace. Wipe the inside of the rim with a wet paper towel.

8. Seal the jars with lids and bands to finger-tight, not snug. Place jars in boiling water canner for 15 minutes.

9. Transfer jars to a towel covering the surface to cool. After each jar has sealed, remove bands and wipe jars clean. Towel dry the lids, jar threads and band threads. When dry, screw the bands back on the jars to lightly tight.

ANY-WAY-YOU-LIKE'EM PORK CHOPS
with
SPICED PEACH CHUTNEY
and WARM POTATO SALAD
from Chef Andy Knudson

Is there anything better on the planet than pork and peaches? Well, maybe pork and apples, but that is what everyone else does. Try this, go to your local butcher and get the pork chops that you are most comfortable cooking. You can master them on the grill, in the oven, or even fried. Any way you like'em is how you should cook the chops.

Once you have those pork chops cooked to your liking smother them with the spiced peach chutney! You just can't mess this up. This is best served with warm potato salad.

Warm Potato Salad

15	boiled fingerling potatoes (sliced)
12	cherry tomatoes roasted in oven for 15 minutes at 350
1	tsp dried oregano
8	fresh basil leaves torn in to pieces
1	tbsp sherry vinegar
1	tbsp olive oil

Mix everything together and make sure you are happy with salt and pepper. Keep this dish warm in oven until you ready to have it accompany the pork chops. Note, this potato salad is really great cold too!

MINTY GREEN APPLE CHUTNEY

Minty Green Apple (green). Talk about green, you have it in this one. The herbs make the apples minty with the tangy, citrus flavor of cilantro. The light crunch of the apples and candied pecans layer the harmonizing textures, making this a clear piquancy pick—a winner! Makes 12 pints.

Ingredients

- 6 cups Granny Smith Apples (six large apples)
- 2 cups sliced sweet onions
- 4 stemmed Serrano peppers
- 1 cup golden raisins
- 3 cups light brown sugar
- ½ cup minced garlic
- ¼ cup lemon juice
- 1 tablespoon ground ginger
- 4 cups loosely packed mint leaves
- 1 cup loosely packed cilantro (with stems)
- 3 cups white vinegar, divided
- 1 cup candied pecans

Steps

1. Peel the apples and cut them into chunks. Stem and cut the peppers into pieces, retaining the seeds for the amount of heat desired.

2. Cut and peel onions; slice in half and cut each in half again. Cut into ¼-inch slices widthwise. A mandolin slicer can be used, but always use this helpful utensil with extra caution. The onions will cook down more like string slices than chunks.

3. Put the peppers, onions, raisins, brown sugar, garlic, lemon juice, ginger and pecans in a stockpot with one cup of vinegar and cook until the onions soften. Add the apples.

4. Put the mint and cilantro in a blender with the remaining vinegar to blend into a green, pasty liquid. Add the mixture to the stockpot and bring it all to a boil. Cook until the apples are soft but still crunchy.

5. Ladle hot chutney into hot, sterilized pint jars, leaving ½ inch headspace. Wipe the inside of the rim with a wet paper towel.

6. Seal the jars with lids and bands to finger-tight, not snug. Place jars in boiling water canner for 15 minutes.

7. Transfer jars to a towel covering the surface to cool. After each jar has sealed, remove bands and wipe jars clean. Towel dry the lids, jar threads and band threads. When dry, screw the bands back on the jars to lightly tight.

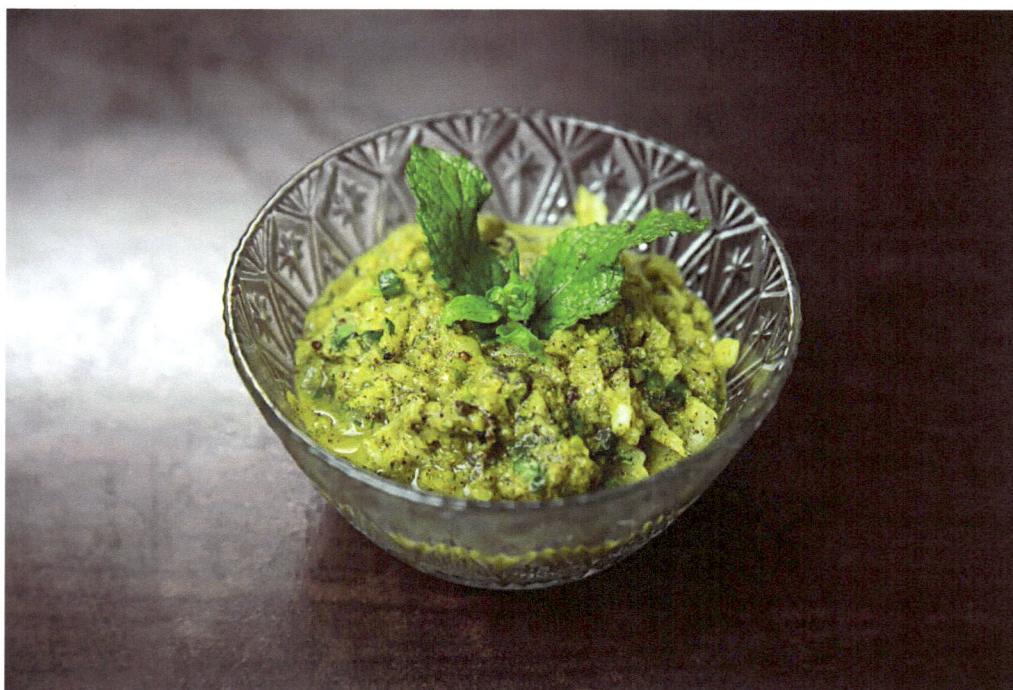

GRILLED LAMB T-BONES
with
MINTY GREEN APPLE CHUTNEY
and INDIAN BASMATI RICE
from Chef Andy Knudson

Lamb cut into T-Bones is meat that we love to eat at home. Reminds me of being with my family, and always asking Mom why she got the lamb cut up when she usually got a rack of lamb. Moms are usually right; the lamb T-Bones char so nicely on a hot grill.

Chef Tip: season the T-Bones to your preference (I prefer just salt and pepper) about an hour before cooking them. This takes the chill off of the meat and they will cook more evenly on the grill.

Cook these babies over a hot grill to the doneness that you like. Place them over a bed of Indian Basmati Rice and pop that jar of Minty Apple Chutney. Now go to town!

INDIAN BASMATI RICE

Ingredients

1 ½	cup	basmati rice
2	tbsp	vegetable oil
1/2	tsp	ground cinnamon
1/2	tsp	ground cumin
1/4	tsp	ground cloves
1/8	tsp	ground cardamom
1 1/2 tsp		salt
2 1/2 cups		water

Place the basmati rice in a medium sized bowl, covering it completely with water. Let it sit for 20 minutes, and then drain the rice. Doing this is going to provide the rice a great texture – please don't skip this step. Heat vegetable oil in a saucepan over medium high heat. Add cinnamon, cumin, cloves and cardamom to the oil and stir until all combined in a saucepan. Add rice to the saucepan and stir until the rice is completely coated with spices (about 2 minutes). Add salt and water to saucepan and bring to a boil. Cover with a lid and reduce the heat to a simmer. Cook for 15 minutes. Remove rice from the stove, and fluff with a fork and serve. Yum!

Story Four

Kindness Connections

COVID-19 was surging, Christmas was coming, and people were dying, but kindness connections were happening.

Deaths of tens of thousands weekly was our national jarring condition in the U.S. as Christmas 2020 approached. It was a surge from Thanksgiving gatherings and holiday happenings. The death toll in the United States was up to 500,000 and was on its way to another 100,000-plus deaths. Close to 4 million people had died worldwide from this mysterious virus. December 2020 was on pace to become the deadliest month of the COVID-19 pandemic in the United States, surpassing April when more than 60,738 Americans were lost. I got sick too.

I found myself absorbing more news than was tolerable, all the while hoping for good news to be coming. Admiral Brett Giroir was part of our congregation and was also a part of President Trump's COVID-19 task force with the likes of Dr. Anthony Fauci, Dr. Deborah Birx, U.S. Secretary of Health and Human Services Alex Azar, CDC Director Robert Redfield, and Vice President Michael Pence.

Admiral Giroir and his wife Jill, mother-in-law Liz Shorey, daughters and granddaughters were all counted among our fellowship. My son Zach and daughter-in-law Emily (a freshman in college and aspiring physician) went on a mission trip with the admiral. I watched their daughters Jacqueline and Madeliene grow up. I had officiated at Jacqueline and Erik's wedding. It was also my privilege to baptize little Isabell and Ellie.

It was an act of kindness that the admiral was available to me to ask questions and seek advice. No one I know is more trustworthy and extraordinarily kind than this consummate health care professional.

The admiral, whom I had always called Dr. Giroir or Brett in less formal settings, was working tirelessly rolling out millions of COVID tests. These tests were crucial in controlling a totally out-of-control pandemic. His work was about saving lives, and he knew the stakes were high. Would he be home for Christmas? The answer was probably not, given the grueling schedule that was consuming him for the good of others. The admiral and his colleagues were walking a political tightrope between sides in our divided country.

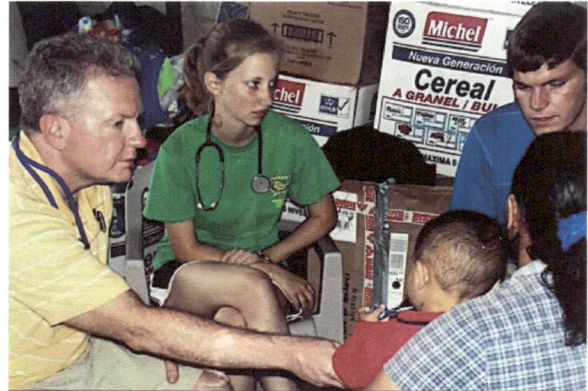

Mask-wearing, social distancing—even testing, and soon we would be throwing vaccines into the crazy mix of political divides. I will never understand how making a case for freedom from masking and vaccinations came to be more important than the safety and care of others and the health of our nation and world—not to mention the economic cost and emotional toll of the fighting factions.

The young woman in green and young man in blue with Admiral Giroir in 2005 both became medical doctors. Who has been your encourager?

I—like all my colleagues—was dealing with this divide in our churches and hearing stories of family members not speaking to one another. All the while, some of us were foolish enough to try to quell jarring hate-talk on social media that was out of control. These were good people with whom I had never witnessed their political opinions becoming their main agenda; it was like a golden calf. Relationships with friends, family, church, science, and even with their parson seemed to be taking a back seat to the placement of oddly defined freedom wrapped in a new brand of nationalism.

Christmas Closed Doors

Hospitals across the U.S. were becoming overwhelmed, and people were dying in record numbers. Even as U.S. and state officials rushed to get lifesaving vaccine doses across the nation, the shadow of death was getting darker. December was already the second-deadliest month of the pandemic in the U.S., as of December 17, 2020. The next day I tested positive, with flu-like symptoms—no energy, low grade fever, and chills. Worse, I was having the familiar ponderings concerning where my illness would go from there.

It was clear that starting to hold in-person services at the church in October was premature. Also, we could not conduct live Christmas Eve services in 2020, which was a first in our 75-year history. Though we knew of no one who contracted COVID-19 in worship during our brief reopening and we were good to wear masks, it was getting dangerous again to gather. Closing would be understood by most but result in angering some—even to the point of them leaving a fellowship that had been so vital to them for years. The hard choice was that we simply would not contribute to the spread of the deadly virus by continuing to meet in person. The doors of the church closed again to in-person worship, and livestreaming was the order of the day.

Fortuitously, when the decision was made to close, we immediately recorded my Christmas Eve sermon in the middle of the day on December 15. I preached to all-too-familiar, lifeless cameras in an empty sanctuary. I could only imagine the sanctuary full of smiling-faced worshippers with hundreds of candles being lit, one at a time, wick by wick. Best of all, the accumulated flames illuminated the room, filling it with stained-glass colors. The entire image brought a peace that I always looked forward to and especially needed this Christmas.

By Christmas, several staff members were sick, my wife Tammy had tested positive, and we were hearing of deaths within the congregation. The dying were mainly among our elderly saints—who we were not allowed to visit.

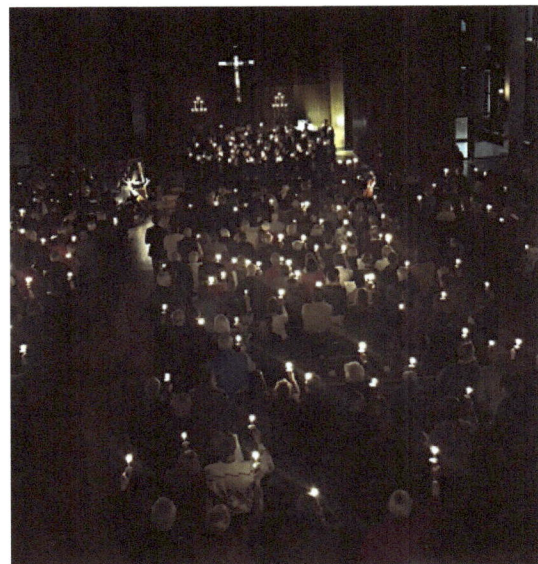

People were dying alone at Christmas time, which just wasn't right. It was so jarring. Across the country, families were still making Christmas plans to gather, regardless of the risks. There were no plans for Christmas with the Copeland family gathering, since Tammy and I were quarantining at home for nearly all twelve of the days of Christmas. January was destined to be even more deadly because of choices made regardless of danger, but the advent of the vaccine was ushering in an epiphany of hope.

A Prayerful Confidant

On a weekday, in a pew at the back of a poinsettia-filled sanctuary, a friend paused as he often did to pray. Billy Bob Harris prayed in a cavernous room empty of people but full of poinsettias that many saw virtually, but few had seen in person.

We had again celebrated the birth of Jesus, but my how the world longed for joy. There was no singing, and there was no "merry" in this Christmas this year. Only the powerful old nativity story—full of purpose and meaning—was whispering hope in our ears, as our eyes gazed on poinsettias of vibrant red and green.

During a jarring, often lonely Christmas, Billy Bob prayed. Every parson needs a person like him, one who loves unconditionally, and you can talk to about anything. He always calls me "Brother Stan," as it was customary in his little Texas panhandle hometown of Gruver to call the parson "Brother."

He is one of the best known of Dallas citizens. He was a very successful stockbroker with his own radio show and a fan base that he delighted in, as they did in him. He is a people person, networker, and connecter. His name has been recognized by many in Dallas for years. To those who know him, they know that there could not be a better friend or a kinder person. A true man of the town back in the day, he often brought his dates to church. Not so much anymore does he bring a date with him to church, but he rarely misses the privilege to worship and is always sharing invitations to others to visit us.

Once upon a time, nearly three decades ago, Billy Bob's life too was jarred through a federal conviction. Months of prison time and loss of his broker's license was his sentence. After a short time away with everybody loving and pulling for him, he came back stronger and deeper—more spiritual than ever. The word that comes to mind when you think of his relationship with others is "beloved." The word that comes to my mind when I think of this great friend is "kindness."

I was once confiding in him, as I do when I get lonely and feel like there is really no one who needs to hear the parson's problems. I was somewhat apologetic to have to be sharing what I would want no one else to hear. He said, "Brother Stan, you can tell me anything and know that it is completely private. Hell, you know I went to prison for not talking."

All the particulars about his white-collar conviction I've never really wanted or needed to know, because I know the goodness that is Billy Bob. The beauty of our relationship is that he comes to me with his challenges as well. I only hope this parson is half the help to him he has been—and continues to be—for me.

It Started with Prayer

I have no doubt I was on his list that day he prayed among the poinsettias. That day he also prayed for his neighbor Lara Burnside. She is a hospital administrator at a well-known Tarrant County hospital—John Peter Smith or JPS Hospital—in Fort Worth, Texas. She makes the drive from Uptown Dallas to Fort Worth daily.

Throughout those days of caring for her staff of health care heroes with COVID-19 raging, whether she made it home at night was part of the fluidity of her predicament. Often during those unsettled times, she spent the night among the nurses. Once when circumstances were dire, she rolled up her sleeves and did hospital laundry all night with the skeleton staff assigned to that task.

She too had found a concerned friend and confidant in her neighbor Billy Bob. He is one who when he says he'll pray for you, he does just that. He once told me that his father, J.C. Harris, was a spinner of folksy wisdom. He said, "My father told me a thousand times, 'Son, pray for me…I need the prayers, and you need the practice!'" J.C.'s son walks the walk and doesn't need to talk the talk. He always prays the prayers that change his life and the lives of countless others.

> *Who comes to your mind who needs a pick-me-up gesture of kindness? What will you do about it?*

He is a talented and gifted connector and has several close friends who are famous performers. He called his multiple-award-winning friend Larry Gatlin and told him about the nurses at JPS Hospital. Larry did a video recording with a message of hope and, of course, a song. The nurses absolutely loved it. Larry too would do just about anything that Billy Bob asked him to do, especially if it was extending kindness to those in need. He is often the one arranging the connection from behind the scenes where he likes to orchestrate kindness.

The nurses' spirits needed a lift—particularly those on the COVID ward, some of whom were staying in hotels to protect their families. He wasn't done praying for those nurses and listening to the One to whom he prayed.

Poinsettias Finding a Home

An idea surfaced as Billy Bob was praying in the sanctuary, upon learning the fate of the 2020 poinsettias that decorated the beautiful space. In normal times, the red floral beauties would be taken to nursing homes and church members in hospitals. Properly cared for, poinsettias will live for months and share the joy along the way. With still no admission to nursing homes and hospitals for visiting clergy, these Christmas staples were destined to be discarded with the trash.

He thought as he prayed, "It is a shame to be just throwing these poinsettias away." Not coincidentally, Lara then entered his thoughts. He did as he often does, felt the nudge from the One to whom he prayed and called Lara. He asked her if she could use a hundred or so poinsettias at the hospital. She was moved by this one more act of kindness. All she could see was her cast of health care heroes, tired and now grieving the COVID death of one of their own. She said, "Sure, I would love to give them to the nurses."

Few of us can fully appreciate the jarring weight of death and dying that health care professionals experience. For the better part of a nonstop, long, surreal year, they had been caring to the point of being nearly all-cared-out. Lara shared with Billy Bob a story about which more of us would become keenly aware. At JPS Hospital, a nurse contracted the disease while caring for another, and the heroic nurse died. The loss of nurses and doctors who paid the ultimate price while caring for others had been publicized for months, and now, the loss of a colleague hit close to home.

A few days later, he met Lara in a mostly empty church on a dreary, rainy Saturday. A van from the hospital pulled into the parking lot. A couple of guys lumbered out of the van to load poinsettias that were as beautiful as they had been portrayed. Tears welled up in her eyes, more prominently accentuated than usual due to her mask. A masked Billy Bob asked if she could use a hug. Carefully they hugged, which was another simple act of kindness that had been in low supply for months.

She then said to him, "I have to thank somebody." He explained that the staff on hand was minimal, but perhaps they could find someone still there on a Saturday. "Trusty Rusty"—Rusty George who is in charge of LLUMC facilities—and a couple of his cohorts were present and accounted for. They heard Lara's expression of gratitude. She was also asked by her caring friend to share what was going on at the hospital and the plight of the heroes there. Tarrant County's numbers were the worst in the state, and the end was not in sight. The weight upon those closest to the front lines of the war on this killer disease was heaviest for nurses and doctors, along with their families.

Prayer Shawls

Upon hearing the larger story from Lara about the toll the pandemic was taking, Rusty said, "Come with me." He took her to a room as the rest followed, to the closet that housed dozens of prayer shawls. These shawls were knitted by a group that used to gathered weekly to knit them. For months their knitting, purling, and praying was done alone in their homes.

The closet was full of prayer shawls. It was shared with her that LLUMC makes those shawls available for free to people who want to give them to a family member or friend or someone we've heard needs prayer, relief from jarring experiences. We have mailed them to Orlando families after the Pulse nightclub massacre. We sent some to contacts in El Paso after the shooting there, to have them placed in the arms of grieving loved ones. Soldiers being deployed have received prayer shawls to keep nearby, reminding them that someone is praying for them. Then Rusty said, "Billy Bob here is one of our best givers of prayer shawls and prayers." She said, "I knew that he must be."

In true Billy Bob form, he deflected the praise to talk about the goodness of his church and its many ministries.

Rusty asked Lara, "How many do you need?"

She said, "I could take one to the family of the nurse who died."

"No Lara, how many do you need?" Rusty repeated.

With tears in her eyes, she said, "Can I have twenty?"

The quick reply was, "Do you want forty? Because our Knit, Purl and Pray team would be most blessed if you took them to the nurses."

She nodded affirming the kindness. Lara—this senior vice president, chief of experience and strategy of a top-rated Texas hospital—was so touched. So was everyone in the room. She said, "I have never received a welcome like this from a church." With some pain in her voice she said, "The last two churches we were a part of were not good experiences. We felt far less than welcome. In fact, the last church asked us to leave." A pregnant pause followed, as tears streamed and moistened the masks of all, but no one asked "Why?"

She was embraced mask-to-mask by several, and then Kathryn, the leader of the prayer shawl pack said, "Please let us pray for you." It wasn't the parson suggesting, it was one of his kind flock. When the beautiful prayer was over, Lara got the same men who loaded the poinsettias to help her with the prayer shawls, including one the group insisted she take for herself.

Winter Pandemic and Hope Coming

The winter gave us reason to need prayer shawls. Christmas gatherings across the country had given rise to another surge in the pandemic, just as the medical experts had predicted. It was the middle of January when I found myself talking on the phone to one of our members who was battling COVID-19. With each call, I knew his jarring fight was becoming tougher. Calls became texts, with his responses "Hanging in," "Holding on" and then nothing. As I, his pastor, and his family were hoping against hope that circumstances would change for the better, the worst was before us.

> *Who comes to mind when you think of people who were lost to COVID-19? Who grieves the lost?*

My next call was from his devastated wife who was asking me to call him one last time before he was to be taken off the ventilator to succumb to the killer virus. It was a first for me. To pray over the phone with one who was about to die, as a nurse held the phone to his ear, was an experience that left me empty.

The family was broken as I also spoke and prayed with them, and so was the nurse who had seen an unfathomable number of scenes like this one. The weight was so heavy. How many scenes like this one had Lara witnessed and heard the despair of her nurse colleagues who were at their wits' end? They were all prepared for so much regarding rendering health care, but not for death on this scale.

February saw a surge in vaccinations, which were just becoming available to the larger public. Tammy and I got our shots as soon as we could make it happen. The miracle of medicine was starting to unfold, and hope for the breaking dawn of a new day of health and well-being was before our eyes. Then jarring news came that Lara was sick. Not with COVID-19, but another acute situation that was said to be serious and might involve emergency surgery. Of course, a masked Billy Bob visited her and sent me a photo with a text, "Brother Stan, Lara's going to be okay. And Brother Stan, she's sleeping with a prayer shawl wrapped around her. God-a-mighty, God is good."

Freedom in Acts of Kindness

When perspectives are changed through relationships, connections, and acts of kindness, we are changed as well. We find an amazing freedom waiting to climb into our hearts. It's a freedom that comes from self-sacrifice and an others-orientation that dons a mask, rolls up sleeves, and puts plans on hold to help others. Especially, we pray for those in the health care trenches who were—and are —there for us. It's a selflessly offered spiritual gift of freedom one receives through acts of kindness.

What I love most about picklin' and canning is giving gifts of kindness in the form of pickled or sweet goodness. Picklin' with a purpose involves the giving of a wonderful jar of delight. It is followed by a prayer and a hug to someone who needs all three—a prayer, a hug and a jar of jam; the Picklin' Parson calls this the Holy Trifecta.

I said to picklin' church friends, "Let's make some Strawberry Basil, Blackberry Mint and Blueberry Thyme jams for all of the nurses at JPS. Let's remind them that we are still here, and they are still heroes and always will be." We love the connection made that changed us in the middle of a time when we often wondered if life in the throes of COVID-19 could ever be redeemed.

Jarring is totally transformed in meaning when it is the process of containing the jams that we will share. Herbs produce an odd savory flavor that most of us adore. The savory and sweetness of the jam is the perfect statement of kindness we always want to deliver. Each jar's label states our slogan: "Loving ALL." I have experienced and witnessed others being set free. Free indeed! Even through the art of picklin' and canning, freedom comes as a gift when offering kindness is the purpose.

I relentlessly hope that Christmas this year will see a return to kindness like we have never seen before. Tables will be set with poinsettias and prayer shawls will be close at hand. Families will be talking about the things that really matter, and the freedom that comes from loving one another. I hope for healing to be in the air, prompting the mending of relationships and forgiveness of past hurts.

Text message: *"Brother Stan, look at this photo of our church that I just took after the storm. Is that not beautiful or what, Brother Stan."* Billy Bob

Try A Little Kindness

If you see your brother standing by the road
With a heavy load from the seeds he sowed,
And if you see your sister falling by the way,
Just stop and say, "You're going the wrong way."

You've got to try a little kindness,
Yes, show a little kindness;
Just shine your light for everyone to see.
And if you try a little kindness,
Then you'll overlook the blindness
Of narrow-minded people on the narrow-minded streets.

Don't walk around the down and out;
Lend a helping hand instead of doubt.
And the kindness that you show every day
Will help someone along their way.

You got to try a little kindness,
Yes, show a little kindness;
Just shine your light for everyone to see.
And if you try a little kindness,
Then you'll overlook the blindness
Of narrow-minded people on the narrow-minded streets.

Composed by Bobby Austin and Curt Sapaugh
Sung by Glen Campbell
Try a Little Kindness lyrics © Beechwood Music Corp., Glen Campbell Music Inc.

From-the-Farm Gourmet

Jams & Jellies with Herbs

/ˈ(h)ərbz/

1) Any plants with leaves, seeds, or flowers used for flavoring, food, medicine, or perfume.

2) Any seed-bearing plants that do not have a woody stem and die down to the ground after flowering. The banana plant is the world's largest herb.

3) The leaves that are put in East Texas berry jams that make them lip-smacking good and add pizazz to whatever they are added to.

So, What's the Difference?

What is the difference between jam and jelly? The answer in a word is "stuff." Jam has the stuff of the fruit that has been mashed where the texture is still apparent, but the fruit is not whole as it is with preserves. Jelly is the strained juice that has no stuff, no pulp—the clearer the better. Cheesecloth is often used to reach this purity for the juice that makes jelly.

Sugar is also a staple in the making of jams and jellies. The riper and sweeter the fruit, the less sugar is needed—if any at all—in jam. Also, the jams and jellies must jell to be the consistency that is desired. Pectin is traditionally used to get the jelled evenness right. There is pectin that is for high-sugar recipes and pectin for low-sugar jams and jellies. There is also pectin in a powder form, as well as a thick liquid. The directions on these boxes are easy to follow, and pectin is readily available. There is a product that is modified vegetable starch that comes out under several brands that has worked well for me in making jams, but I do not use it in jellies. The product I use for jams is Hoosier Hill Farm Clear Jel; for jellies the traditional pectin.

Jam and Jelly Recipes

The two jam recipes and one jelly recipe feature fruit infused with herbs. Matching fresh fruit with fresh herbs is tricky, but success creates a delicate, delightful savory, sweet spread just waiting to make toast, crackers or biscuits come alive. The same can be said for the jam and jelly connections to soft cheeses served as party appetizers.

Currently, we do not grow berries on the Stillwater Farm. However, we are in the thick of berry country. East Texas has lots of large blueberry and blackberry farms. Raspberries are rarer, but new varieties that are more tolerant of Texas climate and East Texas soil have been introduced recently. Add mint to raspberries, basil to strawberries, and thyme to blueberries, and you have a triple dose of herbed berries that is hard to beat.

This craving to experiment with jams and jellies with herbs came by way of the creation of the Sage Blackberry Chutney. It was so good that it encouraged us to explore. We think we have made a great discovery, and you can judge for yourself.

Herb Gardens Can Happen

The parson and his wife Tammy have just put an herb garden in our back yard. One can grow plenty of herbs for berry recipes in a very small, adequately watered, and well-drained space. Herbs are easy to keep, and it is easy to harvest just enough for whatever is cooking—including jams and jellies—in the stockpot.

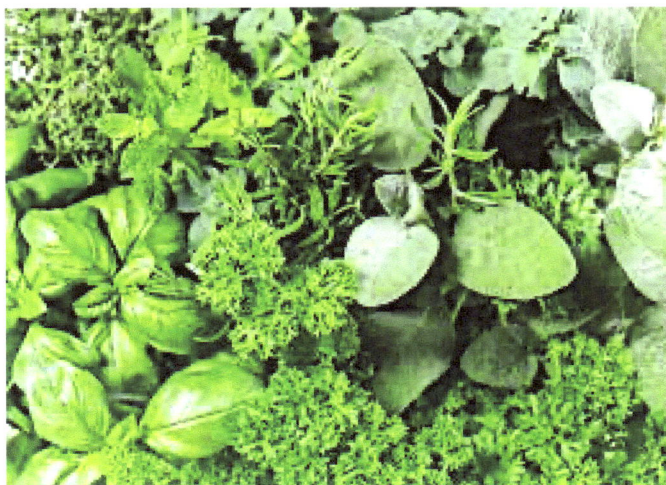

When herbing jam and jelly, add and taste, until you get the flavor that you want. Some like a strong, unmistakable herb taste. Others like mild or more of a hint of the herb. Combining herbs can be tricky, but it can work too. Googling "herbs that are complementary" is a good way to see what herbs are matches and have a chance of making a succulent jar of farm-fresh goodness.

The fun of picklin' and canning is the imagination and creativity that you possess. One reason we call picklin' and canning an art is because it is in the basics that must be learned, repeated, and passed on. Another reason is that it grants a degree of free spirit. A recipe points the way; it does not have to be followed exactly. Many cooks consider recipes as only guidelines.

Our website will feature recipes, even ones that are sent to us. If you send a recipe to us, and we get your permission to publish it, you'll get the credit. As you know, recipes cannot have a copyright. My belief is share and share alike. I get the importance of proprietary rights when making unique products for sale. I guess Colonel Sanders went to his grave with the secret of the eleven herbs and spices, and the amount of each that made the original recipe a huge winner. Now you can see on the internet all kinds of recipes claiming to be the original "original" and Colonel Sanders is rolling.

Thanks for supporting local farming, hardy eating, and good conversation. We're committed to changing the world one jar at a time. Our 2021 jams and jelly are:

Raspberry Mint Jam
Strawberry Basil Jam
Blueberry Thyme Jelly
And Blackberry Sage as a jam is a winner too.

STRAWBERRY BASIL JAM

Strawberries are a favorite of many people. Basil is Tammy's favorite herb. I put this with Tammy in mind. It has a beautiful bright red color and specks of basil. The flavor is unmistakably herby, but the strawberry sweetness comes through strong to create a perfect balance. This jam won a second-place red ribbon at the 2021 North Texas State Fair and a first-place blue ribbon at the West Texas State Fair in Abilene. I thought this was fitting since Billy Bob is a West Texas product himself. Makes 8 half-pints.

Ingredients

- 8 cups hulled strawberries
- 1 cup packed fresh basil leaves
- 5 ½ cups sugar
- ¼ cup white balsamic vinegar
- Juice of one medium lime
- 1 tablespoon butter
- 2 pouches liquid pectin (3-ounce pouches)

Steps

1. Wash and cut the middle out of the strawberries. The absence of the white pulp at the core makes for a prettier and tastier jam.

2. Combine strawberries, basil, sugar, vinegar, and lime juice in a stockpot; crush lightly with a potato masher to start to release juice. Bring to a boil over high heat, crushing and stirring often.

3. Reduce heat and ladle mixture into a blender four cups at a time, blending for 4-5 seconds to thoroughly chop and mix the basil leaves.

4. Pour into a separate container until all the mixture has been blended, creating a smooth substance with leaf specks throughout.

5. Return the mixture to the stockpot, add butter, and bring to a boil. Stir in the Clear Jel or pectin for 1 minute. Reduce heat to simmer, and skim off any foam.

6. Ladle the jam into hot, sterilized ½-pint jars, leaving ¼ inch headspace.

7. Wipe rims, place lids on jars with a damp paper towel, and screw on bands to finger-tight, not snug.

8. Place filled jars in boiling water canner for 12 minutes.

9. Transfer jars to a towel covering the surface to cool. After each jar has sealed, remove bands and dry the lids, jar threads and band threads. When all are dry, screw the bands back on the jars lightly tight.

RASPBERRY MINT JAM

This is our daughter Emily's favorite, and it is scrumptious. It is a dark red or burgundy with the little white raspberry seeds visible among the green specks of mint. The seeds are soft and not at all crunchy like blackberry seeds. For fans of the herb mint, this is a winner. Makes 8 half-pints.

Ingredients

- 8 cups fresh raspberries
- 5 ½ cups sugar
- ¼ cup white balsamic vinegar
- Juice of one medium lemon
- 1 cup packed fresh mint leaves
- 1 tablespoon butter
- 2/3 cup of Clear Jel or 2 pouches liquid pectin (3-ounce pouches)

Steps

1. Combine raspberries, sugar, vinegar, lemon juice, and mint in a stockpot; crush lightly with a potato masher to start to release the juice. Bring to a boil over high heat, crushing and stirring often.

2. Reduce heat to simmer and ladle mixture into a blender four cups at a time and blend for 4-5 seconds to thoroughly chop and mix the mint leaves. Pour the blended mixture into a separate container until all the mixture has been blended, creating a smooth substance with leaf specks throughout.

3. Return the mixture to the stockpot, add butter, and bring to a boil. Stir in the Clear Jel or pectin for 1 minute. Reduce heat to simmer and skim off any foam as liquid starts to thicken.

4. Ladle the jam into hot, sterilized ½-pint jars, leaving ¼ inch headspace.

5. Wipe rims, place lids on jars with a damp paper towel and screw on bands to finger-tight, not snug.

6. Place filled jars in boiling water canner for 12 minutes.

7. Transfer jars to a towel covering the surface to cool. After each jar has sealed, remove bands and dry the lids, jar threads and band threads. When all are dry, screw the bands back on the jars lightly tight.

BLUEBERRY THYME JELLY

Jelly is more difficult to make than jam. It takes patience to get it translucent. Straining once is usually not enough for the consummate jelly-make This blueberry jelly with thyme is truly delicious. The color of blueberry jelly is dark blue; some might even call it navy blue. So, making clearer blueberry jelly does not have a good payoff. The tiny thyme leaves payoff plenty in taste. It's yummy. In the West Texas State Fair, a first place-blue ribbon was won and it was a contender for best of show. Makes 8 half-pints.

Ingredients

- 2 quarts fresh blueberries
- 4 cups water
- 5 ½ cup sugar
- Juice of 2 lemons
- 2 pouches liquid pectin (3-ounce pouches)

Steps

1. Place the blueberries in a stockpot and crush slightly. Add water; bring to a boil. Reduce heat to medium; cook, uncovered, for 45 minutes.

2. Line a strainer with four layers of cheesecloth and place over a bowl. Place berry mixture in strainer; cover with edges of cheesecloth. Let stand for 30 minutes. When done, the liquid should measure 6 cups.

3. Pour the juice back into the stockpot; gradually stir in sugar until it dissolves. Add the lemon juice to the mixture. Bring to a boil over high heat, stirring constantly. Stir in pectin. Continue to boil 1 minute, stirring constantly.

4. Remove from heat; skim off foam.

5. Ladle the jelly into hot, sterilized ½-pint jars, leaving ¼-inch headspace.

6. Wipe rims, place lids on jars with a damp paper towel, and screw on bands to finger-tight, not snug.

7. Place filled jars in boiling water canner for 12 minutes.

8. Transfer jars to a towel covering the surface to cool. After each jar has sealed, remove bands and dry the lids, jar threads and band threads. When all are dry, screw the bands back on the jars lightly tight.

Story Five

Bless Mr. Incredible—Sam

He's a twenty-year old, lanky, red head today; with a smile as big as Dallas. His life was touch and go when he came into the world. His first 61 days of his life he was in the CVICU unit. Would he ever be alright we all wondered, and prayed to that end? Sam's much better than alright, he's incredible.

How would I describe Sam? First, he's the only child of Denise and Tom, two of our good friends, and church members for the past thirty-five plus years. As their pastor, I heard how much they wanted a child. There is no question that God blessed them with Sam.

Denise and Tom were lined up to adoption a baby from Russia, when news came that Denise was pregnant. Days turned into months, trimesters, and finally Sam arrived on March 15, 2001. For a moment all seemed well. We had barely broken into smiles of joy, when we heard word that something—several somethings—were wrong with him and he needed immediate, life-saving surgery 4 days after his birth. On the very next day after surgery Sam crashed twice and had to be put on ECMO (Extracorporeal Membrane

Oxygenation) this machine took up half of Sam's room, but most importantly it kept him alive.

Dr. Brett Giroir, was a Pediatric Intensive Care doctor at Children's Medical Center of Dallas, Texas during Sam's long stay. Dr. Giroir, informed Denise and Tom that Sam's best chance to survive was to be put on ECMO. Over the years, Brett a fellow Lovers Lane UMC church member, became a friend and every time he saw Sam at church, he could see the progress he has made over the years. Always, in his friendly, approachable way, he would interface with Sam as a miracle child with whom he was blessed to be connected.

Dr. Giroir, became four-star Admiral Giroir in 2018, and the 16th Assistant Secretary for Health. His expertise became recognized on the world stage related to the battle against the COVID pandemic in the US Public Health Service Commissioned Corps, but to Denise and Tom he was the personable, caring pediatrician who advised them and helped save Sam's life.

Being on ECMO was not without side effects, however without ECMO none of us would have ever heard that beautiful voice and been brightened by Sam's big smile. Lots of credit for Sam's life goes to the dedicated medical staff at Children's. The nurses and doctors never gave up, and some were also Prayer Warriors in their own right.

Life supportive equipment was all around, as were the masked faces of doctors and nurses for the first months of Sam's life. Best plans were laid by the doctors and medical staff, and decisions to be made were coming Denise and Tom's way at a fast pace. These were decisions for which no parent could have been prepared. What was to be a time of shear elation, had turned into a time of desperation.

Reaching out to Denise and Tom was easy, but not really. Words were so inadequate, and the temptation to try to fix things with a verbal cocktail would be ill-advised. They to know that we cared, would be here, and were on ready to help—just say the word—but surely we could do more. That's it. The call to prayer went out and we parson-types went into action, alongside many friends and family members.

No clergy responded to the call more compassionately than the Reverend Thomas Dudley Dancer—"Dud" to those of us who knew and loved him. He was our chief pastoral care giver, but this was a special case, and it would require keen attention. The best care giver we had to offer was "the Dancer." No one knew that the care would be for so many days, weeks, and months. Dud didn't know either, but he tireless and lovingly responded, day in and day out even while Parkinson's Disease was beginning to seize his body and mind.

Denise and Tom's reported that Dudley was the constant reminder of the presence of God that was with them. Tom reported, "For thirteen days at 4:30 PM while Sam was on ECMO, they would do a brain scan to check for bleeding on the brain. This procedure took approximately 45 minutes. We all knew Sam's fate if bleeding was detected. We could always count on Dudley being at the hospital during this time. He would be in the waiting room, or pacing the halls praying that there would be no bleeding. Dudley believed in prayer, so we were very blessed daily to hear God's encouraging words through our friend and one of our pastors."

BIC Prayers From the Powledge Unit

Tom, better known as Sam's Dad, was, and is part of a group that I was in called, Brothers In Christ (BIC). In the days of Sam's birth, we met to study and pray, to fellowship and have fun together. No one brought us together around our purpose more than little Sam, Denise and Tom were in our daily prayers for many weeks.

On January 7, 2000 I received a letter from an inmate named Royce, at the Powledge Unit of the Texas Department of Corrections. Royce's letter said in part,

"Several weeks ago, I was struggling with the writing of a letter. Around 11:30 on that Saturday night, I discussed my problem with a Christian friend who listened and advised me to 'write the letter'. I prayed over it that night asking for God's direction. Your Carpe Diem sermon to 'seize the day'—write the letter, make that call you have been putting off—was for me.

My attendance by radio only is a by-product of my incarceration. I arrived here June of '97 after the life as I had known it (as an all-American Dad, three time PTA president, Band Booster president) for the past 49 years collapsed in April '96. I will leave here prayerfully in April 2002.

You and the congregation at Lovers Lane, through the broadcast services have become my local family...I have been a member of the United Methodist church since 1966 and would very much like to be a member. I am a real prayer warrior and my decision has come after much time on my knees. Please advise me of what must now take place."

Following that letter, I began to correspond with Royce. He shared his testimony with me. I wanted to know what put him in the tomb of prison. Why was he there? On March 5, 2000, I shared his letter with Lovers Lane UMC. I said in that sermon, "Royce, hear Lovers Lane's affirmation of you as a member. Today, if we will receive Royce Hall in to membership, say Amen." And everyone in the 8:15 am service, which was the one Royce and the rest of the men at Powledge listened to on the radio, said "AMEN!"

From that point on we became concerned, not as much with how Royce came into prison, but how he would leave and rise into our fellowship. Royce wasn't released in April of 2002; it was four long years later. In the meantime, God used our relationship with him to start an Alpha course at Powledge Unit with 20 men. That course became another, and then another. Then we branched out into several different units. In two decades literally thousands of incarcerated men have come into our BIC fellowship.

When Sam was born with all of his challenges, hundreds of incarcerated Brothers were praying fervently for him daily. Royce would share "Sam reports" weekly in prison, and the men continued to pray. Everybody knew Sam. Tom made a trip to Powledge years later to thank them for their prayer. At that time, Sam was on his way to being a young man.

A Special Young Man

The first time I heard that Sam would be a child with special needs, I wondered just what that meant. By definition, a child with special needs is a child, or a youth who has been identified as requiring special attention and specific necessities that other children do not. In clinical diagnostic and functional development, special needs (or additional needs) refer to individuals who require assistance for disabilities that may be medical, mental, or psychological. The definitions lead us toward a condition, or conditions regarding "needs".

The word "special" leads us toward the uniqueness that so many would come to know and love as Sam. He has always been "special" and uniquely created. He has endured more with bravery and class than most could ever imagine; he's special alright. No one comes to church with a brighter smile than my special friend.

Sometime Sam might shout out a hello that dozens of people might like to imitate, but have inhibitions that preclude such a genuine and honest response. He loves to sing and he has a great voice. He has a mind that memorizes. It's more than unique, it's incredible. He has several animated musicals committed to memory. He recalls the words, does the voices of all the characters and sings all the songs word for word—at the drop of a hat. He often comes to church with his electronic tablet that keeps him busy when the sermon loses his attention, and it always does.

Once I called Sam up to sing, *Jesus Loves Me*. In his pure, beautiful voice, with his red hair glowing amber and his bright smile beaming—he sang every word. It was sweet; it was special. It was incredible. When he was done, the congregation broke out into a spontaneous ovation. He snagged the microphone and said in pure Elvis style, "Thank you, thank you very much." Not many left worship that day remembering what I said, but everyone left with a good dose of joy. They would leave to talk about the day Sam beautifully sang, *Jesus Loves Me*. They talk about it still.

The Hospital Prayer

Life has come with tremendous jarring challenges that Sam faces with bravery and joy. He has had several hospital visits and surgeries. A few years ago, he was in the Shriner's Hospital for Children to correct scoliosis, a surgery to straighten his spine that had crooked through the years. He was told that the surgery would make him several inches taller and he seized on that word. Taller was worth it. The procedure would put titanium rods in his back to correct some of the curvature.

When I came into Sam's hospital room he was being prepped for surgery. His parents were there, as was Scott, our Student Ministry director. Sam was very active in Student Ministry. One nurse was putting an IV in his hand, and he was nonchalantly watching her stick the nettle in his hand. We were all visiting when another nurse came by to tell us we couldn't all be in the room, which was a nice way to say Scott and I were getting booted.

I looked at Sam as his pastor and said, "Do you want to pray?" He said "Sure". We all grabbed hands and I was just about to do my "parson thing", when he started praying very confidently, *"Dear God bless me, and Mom and Dad and Pastor Stan and Pastor Scott. Bless the nurse sticking this thing in my hand and the doctors. God, help my back get straighter and me get taller. And thank you for our church. And God, I'm hungry. And God bless Mr. Incredible. Amen."* Sam does have a thing for superheroes like Mr. Incredible, but to many of us he is the superhero. He's special alright; he's incredible.

When we all opened our eyes, the nurses were wide-eyed amazed. One said, "Sam, that was a great prayer. You may be a pastor one day." We all knew that Sam already was a pastor of sorts. Not one of the nurses expected what they witnessed, and especially for Sam to ask God to bless them. Scott and I were just smiling, along with Tom and Denise, because that moment was SO Sam.

I Can Only Imagine

Stories about Sam are endless, and some are like holy legends. Few who were there would ever forget Everybody's Christmas 2018. For the last decade, a few days before Christmas the church hosted Everybody's Christmas—a celebration that includes a feast, a worship service, gifts of coats chosen by attendees and even Santa Claus. The special guests are about 300 men and women from Dallas homeless shelters. We bused them in from locations all over the city to be with us at what has become a highlight of the Christmas season.

Another group started joining us, at the event—former offenders who had been part of the Brothers In Christ group in prison. The first time this group gathered there was only about a dozen. This reunion featured a report on men who had gotten out prison and a time of holy communion. It has grown every year. Currently nearly 200 former offenders— and always Brothers In Christ—gather after the worship service for a time of worship together. Now, their families now come too. Hearing reports on the weekly activities that Lovers Lane sponsors and the list of men who have recently been released, is a highlight. Communion is always served; the servers are those who have come home in the course of the year. It is so uplifting.

Everybody's Christmas 2018 was special, because of Sam. He was called up to sing. Many of the men remembered praying for him for months after his birth until he was released to go home from the hospital. It was the first time that most of them had laid eyes on him, and there was a buzz when he stood up to sing. He loves the stage, and he had memorized the song by Mercy Me called, *I Can Only Imagine*. Word for word, note for note, he sang from his heart and tears were flowing. Of course, Sam was grinning from ear to ear after his performance was completed. Following the service nearly every man expressed their gratitude to him.

That very night I secured with Tom and Denise a date for him to sing the same song to the entire congregation, including the livestream viewing audience. We would sing together to conclude my Easter sermon. Again, he was perfect, and his song was so moving and inspirational. Thousands viewed it on Facebook and YouTube, as we shared our very own Mr. Incredible with the world.

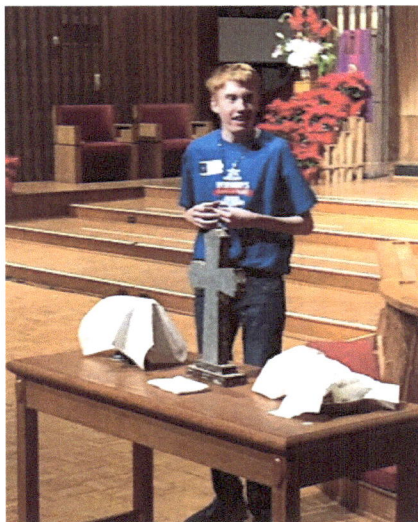

https://www.facebook.com/PastorStan59/videos/10218728666832990

Rays of Light and More

For years the Denise and Tom have been stalwart supports—and Sam a constant participant—in a ministry called Rays of Light. It was a Friday night respite program that takes place at Lovers Lane, UMC campus, as well as it is now offered in two other locations www.raysoflightdallas.org . Special children and youth are coupled with an adult friend, who spends a few of hours with them in play and planned activities. Their siblings can participate too, enabling the parents to have a much needed time together. They go to dinner, or to a movie, or just their more peaceful, less busy, quieter home.

Rays of Light, a Sunday morning partnering program called Austin's Army www.llumc.org/austinsarmy, Deaf Ministry www.llumc.org/deafministry , and several forerunners to these important programs say loudly and clearly that special children are welcome here—all special children. This message is proclaimed to members and guests alike.

There is simply no better ambassador for Rays of Light, and for our church, than the incredible Sam. Lovers Lane has opened the door wide for him to be fully involved in our children's and youth ministries, active in worship and regularly serving as an usher on Sunday mornings. That's why he prays for our church.

Denise and Tom would be the first to say, "Sam has changed our lives, and made them so much deeper and better." They would not be the only ones to speak of the impact he has had on their lives. Friends with Sam in student ministry have a sensitivity to all other youth that would not be as developed were it not for his involvement. Adults who can repeat our mission statement of "Loving ALL people into relationship with Jesus," see that all people come in sacred sizes and packaging— all people, including special children, youth and young adults who come with abilities that are unique and freedoms that are refreshing.

What does the future hold for Sam? Like it is with any of us, it's hard to say. There are things about him that are more certain than most concerning his future. It will be full of animated movies; songs and singing; joyful surprises; freeing, fun and spontaneous outbursts. For he has amazing abilities to memorize scripts that he watches and hears, along with unconditional love that flows to him from others and radiates from within him in a heavenly glow.

Mr. Incredible Apple Butter

Sam is a lover of food—not all food, but the food that he loves he thoroughly enjoys. It has caused me to wonder if picklin' and canning could be in Sam's future. Would he enjoy fruit and vegetables that he especially loves being put in jars to be eaten later, along with jars that could be shared with people he loves? He is a big fan of the avocado, and therefore loves guacamole. Is there a future for avocado in a jar? Is there anyone who would be brave enough to make avocado butter with a savory, sweet taste and a beautifully green color? He just might give it a try.

I have had another thought involving a butter recipe and Sam. I have some natural, no-preservatives-added-vegetable-based food coloring. His most striking feature—aside from his signature smile—is his deep orangish-red full head of hair. My idea is to make some Pear Butter and turn it the color of his beautiful hair. I even have a name for it. This new creation will be called "Mr. Incredible Pear Butter" to those of us who know this story. I sure hope he likes it. God, bless Mr. Incredible—Sam, we love you so much.

Is that Sam behind the mask? It sure looks like it
could be. He is Mr. Incredible. Many of us have
known that for two decades.

From-the-Farm Gourmet
Fruit Butters with Spices
/spīsz/

1) An aromatic or pungent vegetable substance used to flavor food e.g., cloves, cinnamon, ginger, pepper, cumin, etc.

2) A shade of brown.

"I've spiced the stew with cloves, pepper, and fennel seed."

INCREDIBLE PEAR BUTTER

Incredible Pear Butter was created in honor of Sam, Denise and Tom. Pears have a naturally floral taste. This recipe sets out to enhance the floral feature by adding the elderflower liqueur to the butter. The healthy portion of vanilla paste also adds to the floral taste. Fall pears are a family favorite of ours. We have pear trees on the farm that are one hundred years old that were planted by my great-grandfather, Erasmus Cade. To make Incredible Pear Butter, use natural vegetable (no preservatives) food coloring. Red and yellow will get the desired orange. The veggie food color will not impact taste—only color. Think of Sam's hair that looks a bit like Mr. Incredible's hair. Makes 12 ½-pint jars.

Ingredients

- 8 pounds pears peeled, cored, and sliced (Envy, McIntosh, or Gala are preferred.)
- 2 ¼ cups granulated sugar
- 2 ¼ cups packed light brown sugar
- 2 ½ cups apple cider (or apple juice)
- 2 ½ cups apple cider vinegar
- 1 cup elderflower liqueur
- 2 tablespoons vanilla bean paste
- 1 tablespoon ground cinnamon
- ½ tablespoon ground cloves
- ½ tablespoon nutmeg
- Vegetable food coloring (natural with no preservatives)

Steps

1. Wash, peel, core, and slice pears, about 6 pieces per pear.

2. Place the pears in a large stockpot with sugar, brown sugar, cider, vinegar; bring to a steady boil.

3. Reduce the heat to medium and cook for 30 minutes; stir regularly until the pears are soft.

4. Ladle pear mixture into a blender or food processor to purée until smooth and buttery. It really cannot be over-puréed, but if it is under-blended then it will have more of a sauce consistency than butter.

5. Return the purée to the stockpot and stir in the remaining ingredients: elderflower liqueur, vanilla, cinnamon, cloves, and nutmeg.

6. Continue to cook on medium heat—while stirring regularly—for approximately one hour or until the pear butter is the desired color and thickness. When ready, turn off heat and let mixture settle; skim any foam from the surface.

7. Ladle the pear butter into hot, sterilized ½-pint jars, leaving ¼ inch headspace. Wipe rims, place lids on jars, and screw on bands to finger-tight, not snug.

8. Place filled jars in boiling water canner for 12 minutes.

9. Transfer jars to a towel covering the surface to cool. After each jar has sealed, remove bands and wipe jar lids, jar threads and band threads clean. When dry, screw the bands back to only lightly tight.

HONEY APPLE BUTTER

This is a classic spicy apple butter recipe. The addition of honey adds a nice touch and flavor that certainly enhances the mixture of flavors. The spices are so important to make apple butter coincide with apple-picking season which is in autumn. Though the spices make apple butter relate to autumn, it's good in any season—as all of us know who grew up enjoying toast with apple butter. This butter won a first-place blue ribbons at the 2021 North Texas and West Texas State Fairs. Makes 12 ½ pints.

Ingredients

- 8 pounds apples peeled, cored, and sliced (Envy, McIntosh, or Gala are preferred.)
- 4 medium-size Granny Smith apples, peeled, cored, and sliced, adding a tart flavor
- 2 ¼ cups granulated sugar
- 2 ¼ cups packed light brown sugar
- 2 ½ cups apple cider (or apple juice)
- 2 ½ cups apple cider vinegar
- ½ cup lemon juice
- 1 ¼ tablespoon vanilla bean paste
- 1 tablespoon ground cinnamon
- ½ tablespoon ground cloves
- ½ tablespoon allspice
- 1 cup honey

Steps

1. Wash, peel, core, and slice apples, about 6 pieces per apple.

2. Place the apples in a large pot with sugar, brown sugar, cider, vinegar, and lemon juice; bring to a steady boil.

3. Reduce the heat to medium and cook for 30 minutes; stir regularly until the apples are soft.

4. Ladle apple mixture into a blender or food processor to purée until smooth and buttery. It really cannot be over-puréed, but if it is under-blended then it will have more of a sauce consistency than butter.

5. Return the purée to the pot and stir in remaining ingredients—vanilla bean paste, cinnamon, cloves, allspice, and honey.

6. Continue to cook on medium heat—while stirring regularly—for approximately one hour or until the apple butter is the desired color and thickness. When ready, turn off heat and let mixture settle; skim any foam from the surface.

7. Ladle jam into hot, sterilized ½-pint jars, leaving ¼ inch headspace. Wipe rims, place lids on jars, and screw on bands to finger-tight, not snug.

8. Place filled jars in boiling water canner for 12 minutes.

9. Transfer jars to a towel covering the surface to cool. After each jar has sealed, remove bands and wipe jar lids, jar threads and band threads clean. When dry, screw the bands back to only lightly tight.

CARNIVAL CHERRY APPLE BUTTER

This is a variation on a recipe in the first cookbook called Candy Apple Butter that was inspired by East Texas State Fair candy apples on a stick. The color is the important feature with this apple butter as well. The addition of a healthy portion of pitted cherries, along with the dark cherry Jell-O, leaves no doubt that the flavor is cherry and the color is deep, dark red. Makes 12 ½-pint jars.

Ingredients

- 4 pounds apples peeled, cored, and sliced (Envy, McIntosh, or Gala are preferred.)
- 8 cups pitted cherries
- 2 ½ cups granulated sugar
- 2 ½ cups dark brown sugar
- 2 ½ cups apple cider (or apple juice)
- 2 ½ cups apple cider vinegar
- ¼ cup lemon juice
- 1 ¼ tablespoon vanilla bean paste
- 1 tablespoon ground cinnamon
- ½ tablespoon ground cloves
- ½ tablespoon allspice
- ½ tablespoon cayenne (to taste for heat)
- 2 large boxes (3 oz.) black cherry Jell-O

Steps

1. Wash, peel, core, and slice apples, about 6 pieces per apple. Wash and pit the cherries.

2. Place the apples and cherries in a large pot with sugar, brown sugar, cider, vinegar, and lemon juice; bring to a steady boil.

3. Reduce the heat to medium and cook for 30 minutes; stir regularly until the apples are soft.

4. Ladle apple/cherry mixture into a blender or food processor to purée until smooth and buttery. It really cannot be over-puréed, but if it is under-blended it will have more of a sauce consistency than butter.

5. Return the purée to the stockpot and stir in the remaining ingredients: vanilla, cinnamon, cloves, allspice, cayenne, and dark cherry Jell-O.

6. Continue to cook on medium heat—while stirring regularly—for approximately one hour or until the apple butter is the desired color and thickness. When ready, turn off heat and let mixture settle; skim any foam from the surface.

7. Ladle the cherry apple butter into hot, sterilized ½-pint jars, leaving ½ inch headspace. Wipe rims, place lids on jars, and screw on bands to finger tight, not snug.

8. Place filled jars in boiling water canner for 12 minutes.

9. Transfer jars to a towel covering the surface to cool. After each jar has sealed, remove bands and wipe jar lids, jar threads and band threads clean. When dry, screw the bands back to only lightly tight.

Story Six

Everlasting Arms

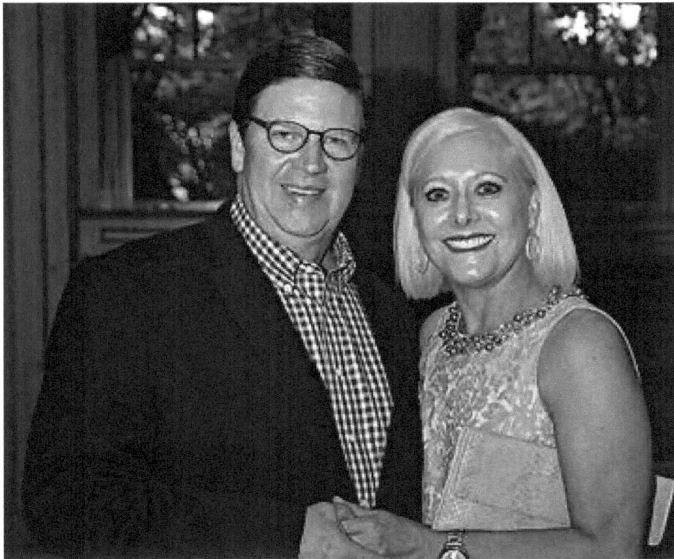

"When you've made it through cancer to the other side, you can get overwhelmed by your debt of gratitude. You can never repay those to whom you feel indebted; you simply pass on the goodness."

A cancer survivor shared these words with me from her own experience, and she is only one to whom I am indebted. I have tried to follow her advice. For more than three decades, I have attempted to pass goodness on to others and offer my story in this spirit. My story is about the most jarring experience of my life. The mystery of how I am here to recount some of the journey makes me scratch my head in wonderment. I have chosen to give science a great deal of credit for my cure and am indebted to God for the healing.

We parson-types do not shy away from the word "testimony" as it relates to personal story. Testimonies are not laden with "shoulds" or "oughts," compelling a "must" of seeing things exactly alike. Rather, testimonies speak like so: "This has been my experience, and this is what, by faith, I believe." Testimony opens us up to the uniqueness of our own personal journeys, and the things we come to embrace as truth along the way. My story is testimony, and I will share what I have come to see as truth in this context.

Community, Family and Grace

If anybody had a Mayberry RFD Andy Taylor upbringing, it was me. I grew up in the rural East Texas town of Chandler when the town population was a few hundred, and it seemed my family was kin to half the citizens there. I referred to "aunts" that really were my aunts and "cousins" with whom I shared no DNA. Chandler was community and family-like with very little disturbance to its harmony. Today, I count all this togetherness as a blessing; the arms of community enveloped me.

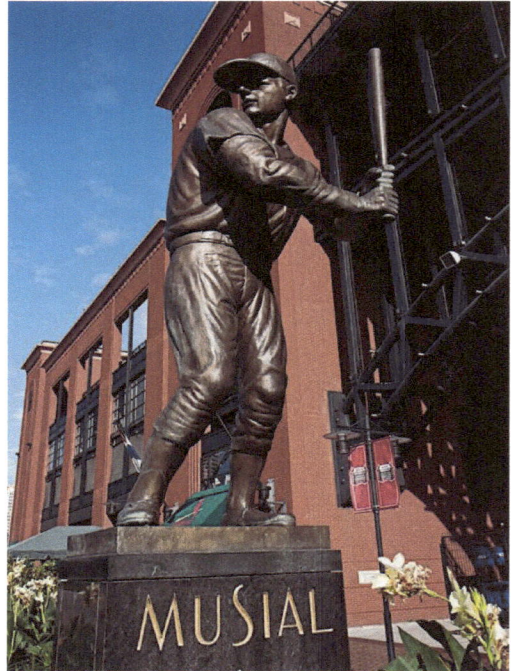

My name is Stanley Reagan Copeland, but I am known as Stan to most. When I was a boy, a few old-timers would often refer to me teasingly as "Stan the Man." There was some truth in that nickname, due to my dad being a dyed-in-the-wool St. Louis Cardinals fan before the Texas Rangers and Houston Astros came to be. When Dad was growing up, it was during the reign at the plate of Stan "the Man" Musial. My dad—like many a kid who grew up in the 40s and 50s in East Texas towns—loved sports. So, it is no surprise that I would be named after one of his sports heroes.

Reagan is my middle name, but not after the once-governor of California and past President of the United States. It is my mother's family's name. My grandfather was named after his mother's family—Clifford. My father was named after his mother's family—Cade. One can probably guess why our son Zachary has the middle name of Barnes. Family tradition is essential when family is important.

I knew my Reagan great-grandparents. In fact, I knew two of my great-great-grandmothers, three of my great-grandmothers, two of my great-grandfathers and my maternal and paternal grandparents, literally, helped raise me. The meaning of "It takes a village" was my reality long before the phrase became cool. Zachary was a teenager and Emily was six when their great-great grandmother, Mamma Reagan, died. She was 102 years old. People in my family live a long, long, long, time.

It is not lost on me that my upbringing is unusual and getting more so. There is a sense in which I feel like a "triceratops" with a life experience that is extinct. I know too well that many have family experiences that are not like Mayberry/Chandler, instead they are the source of many jarring experiences. That being said, my lot in life of having an incredible family experience around grandparents, aunts, uncles, and cousins is but one more gift that I cannot repay. I did not earn or create the gift of family and am forever indebted to those who made is so. In my part of the country, we call it grace. The arms of my family have always embraced me.

Chandler is the rural setting for me, like both of my parents, both of their parents, and all their great-grandparents. It is a river town close to the headwaters of the Neches River. The first lake on the river is Palestine; not /'Paləstīn/, as in the Holy Land, but /'Paləstēn/ as in the lake and the East Texas town not many miles away. The river flows under a small bridge that marks the boundary between the counties of Henderson and Smith. By the time the river gets to the Gulf of Mexico, it is over a mile wide.

Church As Lifeblood

In my rural community, the churches were its lifeblood. We did not even have a Dairy Queen until I was in high school. A Texas town without a Dairy Queen is less than a small town. The church, believe it or not, was the place of action in town. If it was happening and was social, it was probably going on at the church.

I have never known life outside the church. Many of my enduring life lessons were taught by the church, grounded in the hymn about the "old, old story of Jesus and his love." I do not remember even a word profoundly spoken by one of my Sunday School teachers, but I do remember that every word was wrapped in the message, "Jesus loves me this I know, for the Bible tells me so."

A Methodist pastor during my early years had a lot to do with introducing me to broader and deeper dynamics of faith. To this one I owe more than I could ever repay, his name is the Reverend John Byron Jarratt. In our little church, this forever-bachelor was our pastor, youth director, Scoutmaster, ride to Tyler on a Saturday night, ticket to the football games, friend, and significant light that led me and lots of other folk to faith.

I remember Brother Jarratt loading us up in his yellow Chrysler station wagon. It would hold fifteen kids—unseat-belted of course. He took us to a revival on the same football field where I would later sweat and bleed for the fighting Brownsboro Bears. On that Monday night, I heard a fire-breathing evangelist from Houston give his dramatic testimony. He told of how he was saved from a hopeless life of drug addiction and prison to be a follower of Jesus.

I do not really know what he said, and maybe that is best, but what I do know was that he convinced me that it was time to publicly say "yes" to the God who had loved me all my life. I—along with many of the youth in the area, whether Methodist, Baptist,

Assemblies of God or other—walked down on that field and professed faith in Jesus. It wasn't weird in that day, but the church that brought me up in the faith and the pastor who led me to my vocational call yielded to the testimony of a former offender who could convince youth that they needed to draw a line in the sand and cross over.

> **What was your experience of "church" or "spirituality" when you were growing up?**

At the age of 14 through the encouragement of Brother Jarratt, my walk led me to choose my vocation that was referred to as "a call to preach." On my 16th Christmas, I mustered up the courage to say, "I believe God wants me to preach." I preached my first sermon, "Love Came Down at Christmas" in my home church that Sunday night after Christmas. It was five or so awful minutes of sermon, but you would have thought I was Billy Graham, the way the people made over me. I could feel the enthusiastic support of my call. I've carried those memories with me on the journey.

School, Marriage, a Church, and a Baby

After graduating from high school, my college experience was all with the firm understanding that it was readying me for pastoral ministry. At the age of twenty-two, I entered Saint Paul School of Theology in Kansas, City, Missouri. I didn't go to Kansas City alone, however; I had met Tammy Barnes eighteen months prior. We married on May 23, 1981, a few days after I graduated, a few days after my birthday. I was twenty-two; Tammy was twenty-years-old.

I was ordained along the way and after graduating from seminary, I was appointed to "heaven"—First United Methodist Church of Henderson, Texas. It was Mayberry all over again. This church was a loving church and put up with, loved, and embraced me and my ministry. Everything I was called to do as a youth and had been getting ready to do through years of education, I was finally doing—preaching, weddings, funerals, teaching the youth, counseling the adults, and more.

It was at the community drugstore where the daily coffee klatch gathered. It was a group of older men; they first made me aware of the "killjoy" reputation of the clergy. When I walked in, someone half-jokingly would say, "Clean it up men. The preacher's in the room." It is strange how that made me feel so important. It wouldn't be long before they would resort to their cursing, dirty jokes, and racist references. This made me wonder if I could possibly make a difference in this community, but I came back daily for the same dose of reality.

Something else happened in Henderson that was a great blessing. We became parents. Zachary was born and life was different. How could this little guy change so much about life for us? It was a great time. Even our Labrador Retriever had pups. I remember telling Tammy that having kids and pups was so much fun that every year it would be nice to either have a baby or a litter of puppies. Her reply was "I guess we are going to have lots of dogs." Life was so good, and Chandler was just 40 miles away.

The Jarring of a Word

As nearly anyone can attest, our walks are not always smooth and void of bumps along the way. JC Harris would say, "Every path has some puddles." Existence may be Mayberry for a while, but then life happens, and it always happens. Our son Zachary was six weeks old when my life—and consequently our family—was jarred like never before. Quite by accident, through a routine checkup, it was discovered in February 1986 that I had leukemia. It was then that I—like many of you and others whom you love—heard a word that nearly always reorders and unsettles life: "cancer."

I remember it like it was yesterday. Everything I had planned for the weekend and for the future, for that matter, came to a screeching halt. We drove to Tyler and went to Tammy's parent's farm. I went off by myself to have a heart-to-heart with God.

I sat down on a big reddish sandstone rock overlooking a valley surrounded by East Texas hills. There I questioned, cried, prayed, and even shook my fist a little, shouting out, "Why me?" It was one of those deep-valley experiences, a place of decision for me. It was where I tried to balance what I believed was God's call on my life in the face of the struggle to simply live.

> *When was the last time you had to have a spiritual talking to yourself? Do you remember the most poignant time of decision for you?*

In his book *Jesus the Healer*, Dr. Lloyd Ogilvie addresses the need for an inner dialogue, a spiritual talking to yourself, an expression of real thoughts and feelings that must go on. At such a time, many questions tumble into one's mind, and we must talk them out.

Some of the questions were a practical seeking of direction: Should I take a leave of absence? What treatment is right for me? Why did it happen to me? I am young, just twenty-six years old; I am healthy too. How could this happen? People in my family live a long, long, long, time. What went wrong?

This parson had a theological quagmire to work through that I never imagined facing. Applying what I had read about and been trained to do was suddenly a big test of personal reality and theological understanding. How do I pray for myself, for healing? Does

God know or care about my pain? How can God care about individuals with millions hurting? What about those people of faith who prayed and didn't get well? Is there really a God, an afterlife? I proclaim this deity and celestial home at every funeral.

There is so much we just don't know. There were those things by faith that we must declare to know—not by logic or rationale, but by faith. I knew that the Spirit of God was with me as I prayed. I made some decisions that would soon be announced as my new direction. I knew that I decided to live life to its fullest. I vowed to try not to miss a day of ministry, whether that meant for two or three years or a miraculous twenty or thirty years.

When I got off that rock and walked back toward life, I knew I was not alone. I had a real sense of a presence that seemed to say, "It's going to be alright." Ultimately, by faith I could proclaim that I was in God's arms, though the questions would continue to be persistent.

Disease and Treatment

I was diagnosed as having chronic myelogenous leukemia or CML. It is a form of leukemia that has a mutated chromosome which is 100% present in every cell. The chromosome directs the disease to go into a more progressed state. In the 1980s, it was also usually fatal in three to five years. The only real treatment that could possibly cure my disease was a bone marrow transplant. I had no donor, and the odds of success were poor at best.

In June 1986, I was appointed to First United Methodist Church in Houston, the largest United Methodist Church in the denomination. There I could be close to arguably the greatest cancer treatment hospital in the world—The University of Texas MD Anderson Cancer Center. What I found in Houston was ministry like I had never known before. I found that I loved to visit in hospitals, particularly patients who were terminal. I somehow felt myself to be somewhat more trained to hear their fears and feelings expressed from those battling cancer. It was like I was a "cancer cousin" now to so many.

I remember visiting a 38-year-old farmer from Georgia. We had so much in common. He was young, a bit country, a Methodist, had CML, was on the same treatment plan as I was undergoing with the same wonderful doctor. However, he did not respond to the drug and died. Before he succumbed to leukemia, I visited him on what would be his last day on earth. I was so distraught about his situation and feeling what I had only heard about as "survivors' guilt." He said to me, "Stan, I am going to be alright, don't you worry about me. I'll be with Jesus tonight." He was in such peace that it had a powerful impact on me. Part of me wanted to say, "How do you know that?" Another part of me said, "It is so true!" Then he looked me in the eye and said, "You get well. God has plans for you." Again, my mind wanted to question how he knew that, but my breaking heart had me say, "I'll do my best and the best of all is that God is with me. And the best of all is God is with us." I didn't even know what that meant.

I also remember a sermon that Dr. Bill Hinson, my mentor and powerful preacher, proclaimed around the time of the farmer's death. During all my questions, it gave me an assurance that is almost indescribable. He said, "I pray to a God who heals. God desires to heal us and does. Some are healed in such a way that it is inexplicably miraculous, and we are cured. Some are healed through medical treatment and are also cured. Some are healed like the Apostle Paul and live with their 'thorn in the flesh,' but can say God's grace is sufficient to supply all their needs. All of us on this side of the Jordan (on earth) will, ultimately, one day be healed on the other side."

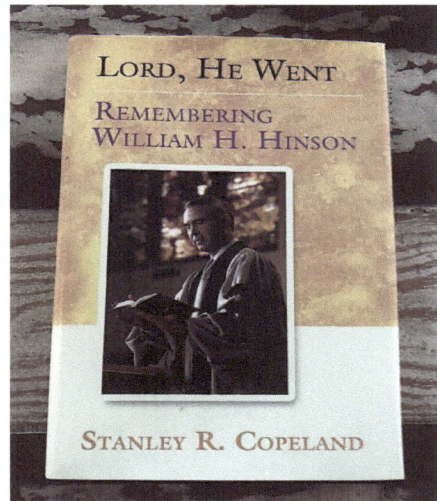

Wow, that was powerful to me! Those powerful words were the foundation of faith on which I began to pray and to center my life. By faith and through prayer I could express the desire of my soul to live and be well, but with the assurance that no matter what happened, I was in God's loving, caring, everlasting, embracing arms. And everything would be alright for me, for Tammy and our little boy. Strangely, I was far from realizing a cure, but I had a sense of being healed. A cure is the redirection of one's body from sick to being well again. A healing is a spiritual matter that involves a deep sense of peace. My farmer friend was not cured, but he spoke to me as a healed person radiating peace.

> "There is none like God, O Jeshurun,
>   who rides through the heavens to your help,
>   through the skies in his majesty.
>   The eternal God is your dwelling place,
> and underneath are the everlasting arms.
>   And he thrust out the enemy before you and
>   said, 'Destroy.'" Deuteronomy 33:26-27
> English Standard Version

In the fall of 1986, I began a five-year treatment taking daily deep muscle injections of the experimental drug Interferon. This genetically engineered drug was a copy of the protein found in our own miraculously created immune systems. The hope was that the drug would interfere with the production of cancerous stem cells in my body. Likewise, the suppressed healthy stem cells would continue production. Over time, the cancer-producing cells would die out. Therefore, a cure was possible? No one, absolutely nobody was promising that.

What do you think about the difference between a cure and a healing? What is your definition of cure? Of healing?

For the record, I believe in science and medicine. My father was a pharmacist. His father was an apothecary who filled prescriptions for the one doctor in our town. I probably would have been a pharmacist if God had not seen my chemistry grades and called me to preach. My sister got the third-generation nod. Let me say it again, I believe in medicine. I believed in this therapy. I believed in my doctors. I believed in prayer.

It was healing to me to know that not only was I praying for myself, but others were praying for me. People prayed for me—family, friends, strangers, friends in other parts of the world, and people I still do not know about. Theologically, I am not of the mind that the numbers of prayers directed to heaven somehow persuades God to pull a string, and you are cured.

Prayer changes us and gives us perspective and peace amid our circumstances. I know how healing works; it is a resolve to be in God's care and everything, ultimately, will be alright. A cure is more complicated, because it involves our imperfect bodies that sometimes fail us. Why are some who we pray for cured and some are not? If you have an answer to that one, try it out on me. It's still a mystery to me.

A Cure and a Lasting Healing

After nine months of treatment and much prayer, I received the first word that there had been a reduction in the cancerous cells. What once had been a 100% mutated chromosome was reduced to 85%. Three months later half of my cells were healthy. Three months later 85% were normal. Three months later 95% were clear of the cancer.

Does prayer change you? How does prayer change your circumstance i.e., sickness, loss, attitude, commitment?

In August 1988, while visiting some dear seminary friends at our annual reunion in Kansas City, my nurse at MD Anderson Cancer Center called me. She said, "Are you sitting down?" I said, "Yes," but every fiber of my being was at attention. Then she said, "We cannot find one cell in your bone marrow with the cancerous chromosome." I cried. Tammy cried. Our friends cried. Later that day, we planted trees. One they planted for me. It was a walnut tree. When I asked why a walnut tree, one of my friends said, "Because a walnut tree lives a long, long, long, really long time."

Subjected to the most sensitive of tests, the doctors have not found in my body—which is filled with millions of cells—even one cell that has a cancerous chromosome. I have heard the word "remission." Through head-scratching wonderment, I have even heard the word "cured." My doctor told me that only 2% of those on the protocol had the result that I experienced. The doctors had officially called it off only two years into the protocol process. The protocol proved that drug to be ineffective in treating CML. My experience was quite unique. Does that make me feel special? Better than most? Not at all? It makes me feel thankful and somewhat overwhelmed by my debt of gratitude.

How could I ever repay my doctor, other doctors and nurses who cared for me, and all those who prayed for me? How can I possibly give gratitude to my wife Tammy who had to take very seriously our vows to love in sickness and health? Every day for five years she gave me an injection. What about my family and friends, who were the constant encouragers? What about God who gave me peace and so much more?

At the end of my five-year treatment, Tammy was pregnant with our second child, a girl. I knew that we would name her after a dear, friend who kept Zachary for at least a thousand hours—Mary Grace Randerson. Grace would be our daughter's middle name and Emily her given name. It was a reminder to me when she was born that "grace" is the most powerful force in life. It is the explanation of the payment of the debts that can never be repaid. It is the gift that confirms that all is made right. By faith we respond best to grace, by living a thankful life, and passing the goodness of God on to others.

> *What do you think about Dr. Kriewald's quote, "The healing power of God is ever present, and Christians should not be afraid of honesty: naming the source of their pain, entering the suffering without glorying or wallowing in it, letting the pain go, witnessing to the power?"*

I will forever be thankful for a little book, another gift of grace called *Hallelujah Anyhow! Suffering & The Christian Community of Faith* by Dr. Deidra Kriewald. It gave me my vision for healing and hope for a cure. She wrote the book after her young husband was tragically killed, and she struggled with anxiety. Words from the book that will always resonate with my soul: *"The healing power of God is ever present, and Christians should not be afraid of honesty: naming the source of their pain, entering the suffering without glorying or wallowing in it, letting the pain go, witnessing to the power."* I've been witnessing to the grace of healing ever since.

Salty Dog Dills look really great with a stained-glass background. Can't say that it helped the Picklin' Parson much.

Leaning on the Everlasting Arms

What a fellowship, what a joy divine,
Leaning on the everlasting arms.
What a blessedness, what a peace is
mine,
Leaning on the everlasting arms.

Leaning, Leaning,
Safe and secure from all alarms;
Leaning, Leaning
Leaning on the everlasting arms.

What I have to dread, what have I to fear,
Leaning on the everlasting arms.
I have blessed peace with my Lord so
near,
Leaning on the everlasting arms.

Leaning, Leaning,
Safe and secure from all alarms;
Leaning, Leaning
Leaning on the everlasting arms.

Songwriters: Elisha A Hoffman/Cyril A
McLellan/A Showalter

AN AMARETTO CHERRY TOPPER

Amaretto cherries made from scratch are almondy, boozy, robust, and delicious. A perfect addition to lots of desserts like cheesecake, ice cream, or an amaretto cherry pie. Savory dishes can include amaretto cherries as well, along with cocktails needing a cherry garnish. Fair. Makes 8 pints.

Ingredients

- 1 gallon sweet, pitted cherries
- 4 cups granulated sugar
- 6 tablespoons lemon juice
- 3 cups Amaretto liqueur
- 3 teaspoons vanilla bean paste or vanilla extract
- ¼ teaspoon bitter almond flavor

Steps

1. Stone the cherries with a cherry pitter. Place them in a large heavy-bottomed cookpot.

2. Add the sugar, stir gently, and bring to a boil. Cook gently for about 15 to 20 minutes; the liquid should start to look like a light syrup.

3. Add lemon juice, Amaretto, vanilla, and bitter almond flavor.

4. Continue cooking for 10 more minutes. Remove the foam.

5. Divide the cherries between the hot, sterilized pint jars and cover them completely with the liquid, leaving ½ inch of headspace.

6. Wipe rims, place lids on jars, and screw on bands to finger tight, not snug.

7. Place filled jars in boiling water canner for 12 minutes.

8. Transfer jars to a towel covering the surface to cool. After each jar has sealed, remove bands and wipe jar lids, jar threads, and band threads clean. When dry, screw the bands back to only lightly tight.

Cookbook Champions

Mary & Jack Balagia
Genie & Jim Bentley
Jane Bever
Carl Box
Darlene & Von Breaux
Kenneth Cade
Tammy & Stanley Copeland
Uel & Margaret Crosby
Sarah & Joe Cutrona
Kay & Karl Dial
Serina & Paul Ditto
Sierra & Matthew Dwight
Mary & Paul Early
Beth Emery
Sandra Estess
Diane Frank
Susan & Woody Gandy
Betsy & Dan Garner
Judy & Jim Gibbs
Miriam Goodwin
Marsha Gordon &Doug Reader
Lisa Hanes
Virginia & Rick Herrick
Anne & Mark Holubec
Nancy Holubec
Mary Kay & Tom Hudspeth
Pam Jackson

Dede & Jeff Jones
Suzanne & Mark Knudson
Claire & Bob Kowalski
Barbara Marcum
Allyson McBride
Traci & Andy Merritt
Amy & James Mills
Becky & David Motley
Batsirai & Ngoni Mukarakate
Shawna Neal
Judy Pollock
Melinda & Scott Powell
Mary Reed
Dana & Ron Rains
Diane & Don Ross
Liz Shorey
Suellen & Joel Stephenson
Alice Swank
Ginny Tenguns
Karen & Patrick Walker
Milton Wallace
Shannon Watson
Mary & Norton Wells
Donna Whitehead
Esther & DJ Wilkerson
Julie & Phil Wilmot
Sara Wyche

Appendix A

Water-Bath Canning

Equipment

Water bath canning is a simple process, and like most anything else, it becomes easier with practice. The equipment is essential, and most of it is part of every standard kitchen. There are, however, a few items that are large and necessary or are specific to the canning process. The investment in the proper equipment saves time and energy, helping to assure the cook that the jars of pickled vegetables, jellies, jams, preserves, and other homemade fruit delights will be handled and sealed properly. It is not an expensive endeavor to obtain the equipment, and it will help the process flow smoothly.

- Large stockpot
- Large canning pot
- Crock #3 or #5
- Large bowl
- Jar tongs
- Jar funnel
- Wooden stir spoons
- Knives
- Peeler
- Corer
- Strainer
- Ladle
- 8-cup measuring bowl
- Measuring spoons
- Mason jars, lids, and bands

Sterilizing

"Clean and hot" is the goal set forth for all jars that will hold the cooked fillings. Sterilizing can be simply washing and rinsing the jars and putting each jar in a large pot of boiling water without the lids and bands. The dishwasher is another good way to get the jars

clean and sterilized. Keeping the jars hot until they are filled is a good practice. Hot filling in hot jars is the optimal way to can, and sterilizing is the next important step.

1.   Preheat the oven to 225 degrees and turn the oven off so it will remain a warm environment for the jars until time to can.

2.   Sterilize jars and lids separately in boiling water for 2 minutes; then remove from the water with jar tongs. The bands do not need to be washed.

3.   Place jars on a cookie sheet with the open end up and place in the warmed oven.

4.   Place lids on a clean towel to air dry, and then wipe dry with a paper towel.

5.   Remove jars from the oven when filling of the jars is the immediate next step.

Filling

After the cooking is done and the creation is ready to be placed in jars for canning, all is ready for the step that requires a bit of careful handling. The most important utensils to have ready for this part of the process are a jar funnel and a ladle. Having a warm, damp paper towel to clean the rims and insides of the jars of any residue is another important necessity in filling the jars. Cleaning the jar threads on the outside of any residue is also important.

1.   Funnel the mixture into the sterilized, warmed jars, leaving ¾-inch headspace on quart, ½-inch on pint, and ¼-inch on half-pint or cup jars.

2.   Wipe and clean threads of jars with a hot, damp paper towel.

3.   Seal the jars with lids, and finger-tighten (not snug) the bands.

Sealing

When all jars are filled and the large pot of water is boiling, all is ready for the final—and most important step—of sealing the jars. Remember to be careful when placing jars in the water using the jar tongs. Keep jars upright. Don't let them tip over and allow jar fillings to coat the upper part of the inside of the jar and lid. The same care should be taken in removing jars from the boiling water. Careful is key. The spillage is not harmful; it's just looks messy and unappealing.

1. Place jars with lids and bands in a large canning pot of boiling water for 12 to 15 minutes with jars fully immersed in the water.

2. Remove jars with jar tongs to a towel-lined counter or a rack.

3. Let jars cool to complete the sealing process. Listen for popping sound as a vacuum is created by the cooling of the jars. Also, lids will not come up when pushed down with a finger if jar is properly sealed.

4. When the jars are completely sealed, after about an hour, remove the band and dry the top of the lid and the inside of the band, reducing the possibility of any rust buildup over time. After completely dry, finger-tighten (not snug) the bands on the threads atop the lids.

NOTE: A properly sealed jar can last in a cool closet out of direct sun for over a year. If any jars do not seal, store them chilled in the refrigerator. Opened jars should last one to two months in the refrigerator. Let sit 24 hours before eating.

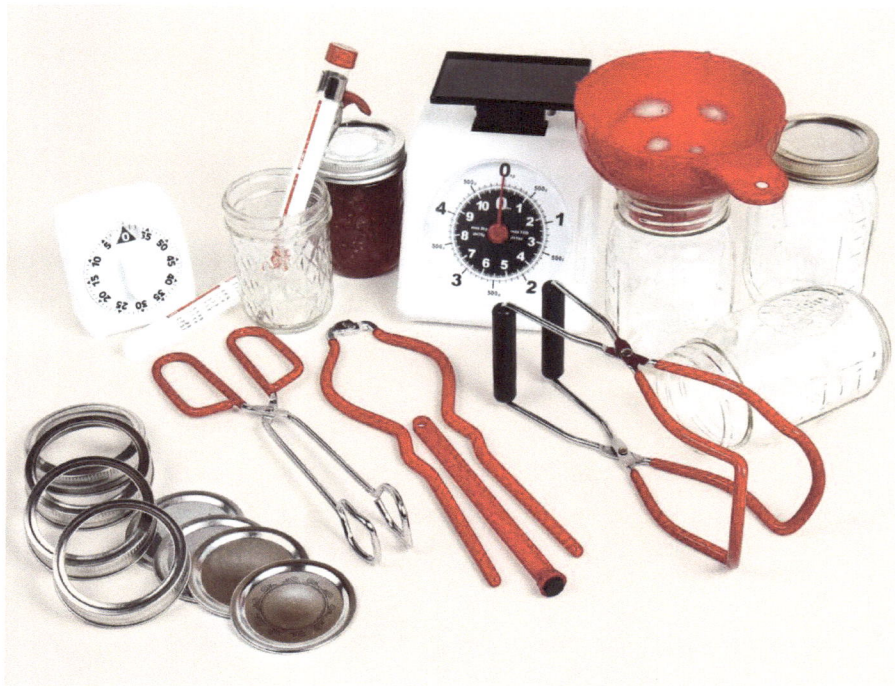

What happens when we live God's way? He brings gifts into our lives, much the same way that fruit appears in an orchard—things like affection for others, exuberance about life, serenity. We develop a willingness to stick with things, a sense of compassion in the heart, and a conviction that a basic holiness permeates things and people. We find ourselves involved in loyal commitments, not needing to force our way in life, able to marshal and direct our energies wisely. *Galatians 5:22-23*

Appendix B

Brining & Crisping

Fermenting (Brining) Pickles

Pickling is the process of preserving food by anaerobic fermentation in brine or vinegar. The process my family used in pickling was brining and is a two-part process. The beginning was a style of fermenting, in essence, with basically soaking for one week in salt water. Though this process perhaps existed in my family for 10 generations, pickling began 4,000 years ago using cucumbers native to India and harvested in the Tigris Valley. This part of the pickling process that my family used was a seven-day process.

Although the process was invented to preserve foods, today pickled foods are made and enjoyed because people like the way they taste. The term pickle is derived from the Dutch word "pekel," meaning brine or northern German "pökel," meaning salt or brine. Of course, brining was necessary before refrigeration to keep vegetables and meats preserved and safe for consumption.

This wet-brining technique promotes the development of lactobacillus—a bacterium that works to break down sugars into lactic acid, a natural preservative. Over time, the vegetables will soften as if being gently cooked and take on a tangy, sour taste.

Our family recipe ratio is 3 cups of salt to 24 cups or 1 ½ gallons of water for any wet brine. If you're feeling fancy, throw in some smashed garlic cloves, peppercorns, citrus (also smashed), or even a sweetener like honey, ribbon cane syrup or brown sugar. The addition of "extras" infuses the vegetables and slightly flavors them. The addition of sweeteners can slightly brown the vegetables.

1. Add 1 cup of kosher salt or sea salt to one gallon of water and bring it to a boil.

2. Pour the salty water over the vegetables that are in a crock. Place the crock lid or a plate on top to make sure vegetables stay submerged.

3. Let them stand in the brine for seven days.

4. Skim the foam that rises to the surface of the brine every evening.

5. I have added a feature of rinsing in ice cold water and letting the vegetables stand in the water for one hour, before returning them to the crock for the crisping stage.

Crisping Pickles

Alum is a chemical compound most commonly found in the form of potassium aluminum sulfate. Alum is added to pickles to create the classic crispness and crunch of a good dill pickle. According to the U.S. Department of Agriculture, alum may still safely be used to firm fermented cucumbers, and it does not improve the firmness of quick-process pickles. The three-day process my family used definitely improves the crispness when followed as outlined.

I have found that using the product Pickle Fresh—which is simply calcium chloride made by Ball and other companies—works just as well. Some old-timers say that grape leaves also produce the crisping. I have not tried the leaf infusion. The process will be shared as was always done in our family; note that using calcium chloride or Pickle Fresh has become my new practice.

1. On Day 8, drain the brine in a place where vegetation will not be impacted; do not pour down the sink.

2. Cut cucumbers into chunks about ½-inch thick or leave them whole, and place in a bath of ice water for one hour.

3. Make a crisping solution with one tablespoon of alum to 1 ½ gallons of water in a large pot.

4. Bring the alum and water to a boil and pour the crisping solution over the pickle chunks that are in the crock while the water is still boiling hot.

5. On Day 9, repeat Steps 1-4 deleting the ice water bath. Drain the brine from the cucumbers. Cut into chunks; no ice water bath is required. Make a batch of crisping solution with water and alum; bring to a boil. Pour it over the pickles while it is still boiling hot.

The last step in the process is the spicing. Our family recipe calls for spicing for three days, increasing the sugar in the syrup by one cup each day. Day 12 is the day the pickles are ready for the jars and the canner.

Claire Bear, Zachary, Emily Grace, Tammy, Emily Marie, Lily Grace, and the Picklin' Parson, and Big Tex say, "Howdy folks, and thanks for reading the cookbook.

www.ingramcontent.com/pod-product-compliance
Lightning Source LLC
Chambersburg PA
CBHW042030090426

42811CB00016B/1800